International Relations
A Concise Introduction

Noah Y. McCormack and Patrick W. Strefford

Introduction: Teaching and studying international relations ········· 4
Outline ········· 5
Chapter 1 Social Science and International Relations ········· 8
　1-1 Change and continuity: perspectives on the past, present, and future ········· 10
　1-2 The three levels of analysis and international relations ········· 13
　1-3 Proximate and underlying causes ········· 15
　1-4 Academic investigation and the problem of perception ········· 18
　Questions ········· 26
Chapter 2: The modern interstate system ········· 27
　2-1 The Treaty of Westphalia ········· 28
　2-2 The centralization of power ········· 29
　2-3 Capitalism and industrialization ········· 32
　Questions ········· 37
Chapter 3 International Relations: history and theory ········· 38
　3-1 Theory in everyday life ········· 38
　3-2 Liberal idealism in the early-twentieth century ········· 40
　3-3 Classical realism in the mid-twentieth century ········· 43
　3-4 Neo-liberalism in the postwar era ········· 47
　3-5 Neo-realist international relations theory ········· 49
　3-6 The international society school ········· 51
　Questions ········· 54
Chapter 4 Realist theories of international relations ········· 55
　4-1 Achieving security ········· 56
　4-2 The Neo-realist theory of international relations ········· 58
　4-3 The effects of realist thinking ········· 60
　4-4 Criticisms of realist thinking ········· 62
　Questions ········· 64
Chapter 5 Liberal theories of international relations ········· 65
　5-1 Progress through reason ········· 65
　5-2 Sociological liberalism: transnational communities ········· 68
　5-3 Interdependence liberalism: free trade and peace ········· 70
　5-4 Republican liberalism: democracy and peace ········· 73
　5-5 Institutional liberalism: international organizations and law ··· 74
　5-6 Evaluating liberal theories of international relations ········· 76
　Questions ········· 78
Chapter 6 Marxist and neo-Marxist theories of international relations ··· 79
　6-1 Modes of production ········· 79
　6-2 Lenin on capitalism and imperialism ········· 81
　6-3 Dependency theory and world-systems theory ········· 83
　Questions ········· 86

Chapter 7 Constructivism in international relations theory ············· 87
  7-1 Social constructionism ··· 88
  7-2 Constructivism in international relations: transformations in the Sinocentric East Asian order ································· 90
  7-3 A constructivist perspective on realist thinking ················ 94
  7-4 Debates concerning the constructivist approach ················ 95
  Questions ·· 99
Chapter 8 Feminist theories of international relations ················· 100
  8-1 Looking at the world through a gendered lens ················ 101
  8-2 Feminist critiques of realism ································· 107
  8-3 Feminist critiques of liberal theories ························· 109
  Questions ·· 112
Chapter 9 Foreign policy and state actors ···························· 113
  9-1 System level factors affecting foreign policy making ········· 114
  9-2 State Level Factors affecting foreign policy making ·········· 118
  9-3 Individual Level Factors in foreign policy making ············ 127
  Questions ·· 129
Chapter 10 Non-state actors in world politics ························· 130
  10-1 Global IGOs ·· 132
  10-2 Regional IGOs ·· 137
  10-3 NGOs ·· 142
  10-4 A non-polar world? ··· 148
  Questions ·· 149
Afterword: Looking back, and looking forward ························ 150

Pictures and maps

Front cover photograph: Apollo 17 image of earth from space, NASA.

Figure 1, Chapter 2 "World map (Mercator projection) Pacific-centric" by Hccbe - Own work. Licensed under CC BY-SA 4.0 via Wikimedia Commons - https://commons.wikimedia.org/wiki/File:World_map_(Mercator_projection)_Pacific-centric.svg#mediaviewer/File:World_map_(Mercator_projection)_Pacific-centric.svg

Figure 2, Chapter 2 "Peters projection, blank" by Peters_projection,_date_line_in_Bering_strait.svg: Lipedia - Peters_projection,_date_line_in_Bering_strait.sg. Licensed under Public Domain via Wikimedia Commons - https://commons.wikimedia.org/wiki/File:Peters_projection,_blank.svg#mediaviewer/File:Peters_projection,_blank.svg

Introduction: Teaching and studying international relations

"Some people dream of success while others wake up and work hard at it."

In this textbook, we aim to provide an introduction to international relations, or in other words, to the academic discipline that specializes in thinking about the political, social, economic, and cultural relationships between the various actors on the world stage. The first thing that we do is review the discipline of international relations as it is conventionally taught today. That is, we explain the main concepts and theories, looking at what kinds of events and trends they are good at explaining, and what they are less good at analyzing. To do this, we refer to a wide range of contemporary and modern examples, and we try as far as possible to refer to cases taken from the East Asian region as a whole, and Japan in particular. This is because the authors are based in Japan and teaching international relations in English to students mainly from Japan and neighboring countries.

Most English-language international relations textbooks are heavily focused either on the United States of America, either on the UK and Europe. Their language tends to be aimed at native speakers of English, and their examples tend to come from a Euro-American cultural tradition. Although many examples are still from the core regions of the world system, in this textbook we try to provide an academic introduction to the discipline that is accessible to students from non-English speaking backgrounds, and relevant to students in the north-east Asian region especially. We have tried to explain the key ideas and theories in straightforward language, and to use everyday examples as much as academic examples.

This textbook's origins are connected with the authors' individual teaching careers, which began in Japan in the 1990s and 2000s. Aiming to further the internationalization of Japan's universities in the post-1980s wave of globalization, many institutions set up courses or sometimes even departments that taught content-heavy

Introduction: Teaching and studying international relations

classes using the English language as the medium of instruction. Recruited to teach in these programs by universities in Kyoto, the authors' task, shared with many colleagues past and present, was to provide social science and humanities classes in English. To do this, we began by using academic texts designed for native speakers of English.

Given that such programs were new, that hired faculty were relatively young and overwhelmingly educated at Australian, North American, and British universities, that there was minimal supervision or input from Japanese faculty, and that most instructors in these new programs were lecturers on fixed-term contracts that did not provide a pathway to tenured positions, we instructors were positioned on the margins of the relatively large Japanese institutions that we taught in. At the same time, and partly because we were not part of the institutional mainstream, we enjoyed a high degree of autonomy in deciding course content and class style.

However, this relative freedom was counter-balanced by some serious problems. For a start, to teach "content" or academic courses to Japanese university students using textbooks designed for native speakers of English was no easy task. One major problem was that students' familiarity with grammar and vocabulary was in most cases not sufficient to read, understand and apply theories and concepts in regular academic textbooks. Even if students had scored well on English proficiency tests or on university entrance exams, their academic English skills were lacking. To present this problem in a different light, the teaching materials that we used were generally unsatisfactory, from the students' point of view.

At the same time, from our point of view, content material set at the level of students' English language ability was too simple. The many textbooks that depend on newspaper-article length annotated texts concerning a wide range of topics may be indispensable as a means of teaching students relatively simple English. But for instructors tasked with providing academic classes at university level, they were lacking in both breadth and depth. This book is our belated response, and an attempt to provide something academic that is at the same time relatively readable.

Outline

To begin, we set out some opening questions that indicate the general directions and concerns of this textbook in terms of its coverage of international relations theory.

First, how useful are so-called realist approaches to international relations, with their focus on increasing state economic and especially military power to achieve national security, in understanding today's global age? What does the apparent regional divide in state strategy between, for example, the European Union, which emphasizes military security less and less, and the East Asian countries on the other hand, which look to boost their military strength more and more, mean? What does the future hold, regarding state strategies for achieving security?

Second, although the post-World War II world was marked by a struggle between the United States and the Soviet Union that could be explained with reference to realist theories, it was also marked, at the same time, by other international trends that could not. The rise of free trade, democracy, international law, and international institutions provide examples of how relationships involving cooperation and mutual benefits also became common. Postwar Japan and Europe provide important examples that support the liberal position, that it is possible to change state behavior for the better, and encourage states to work together and achieve peace and security through cooperation (albeit with the support of the United States).

Today, while international organizations enjoy greater influence than ever before, the power of the Euro-American states seems to be declining, due to factors such as debt increase, ageing, and especially the rapid economic rise of many other states. States such as China and Russia, which are more authoritarian than democratic, and more realist than idealist, are enjoying increased global influence linked to their economic growth and / or military expansionism. In Asia specifically, authoritarian governments exist in China, North Korea and Myanmar, while authoritarian tendencies are visible in Singapore, India, Vietnam and Malaysia, for example. What does the future hold for this region? Will liberal trade policies bring about more liberal political and social policies, as well as more cooperative security systems, or are we entering an era of competitive power politics in the Asian region?

Third, Marxist, feminists, environmentalists, and other activists around the world draw our attention to a wide range of serious global problems. These problems include the massive economic differences that exist both within and between countries, which directly affect issues such as health, education, and life expectancy, and which therefore can be considered to be serious threats to human security. They also include the gaps between men and women in terms of power and security. Feminist thinking has, for example, made clear how realism, which tends to assumed that people are fundamentally selfish power-seekers, can be understood as a theory based on a particularly masculine view of the world, and suggests that security-related strategy and thinking need to be critically re-examined from the perspective of gender.

These alternative theoretical viewpoints on the world suggest to us that the elevation of national security and economic prosperity to the position of primary goals in many societies may have blinded us to broader and more significant issues of human and environmental security. Indeed, what we understand as international or domestic, what we understand as security and insecurity, are things that are constructed in social interaction with others, and so are constantly changing, as constructivist theorists teach us. Investigating the ways in which realism and liberalism became dominant theories in intellectual and political life from a constructivist viewpoint will help us to contextualize their importance, and to consider the significance of these alternative viewpoints on the world. They offer us the possibility of finding ways to achieve more social and economic justice, less environmental destruction and conflict, and overall increases in human and global security.

In the introductory chapter, we set out some of the analytical tools and academic concepts that will help us to make sense of the world, before going on to explain the major theoretical frameworks outlined above. The currently power balance in the academic discipline of international relations tends to be reflected in the fact that states and interstate relations receive the most attention. However, we end this volume with a reminder, that states are not the only important actors, and indeed, that many of their functions may be met by other kinds of institutions in the future.

Chapter 1 Social Science and International Relations

"No one can predict the future exactly, but we know two things: It's going to be different, and it must be rooted in today's world." Peter Thiel

Why is it important to have an understanding of the domain of international relations? Simply put, we do not live in a world of relatively autonomous states. We live in states, which form an interlinked system, joined by shared concerns with economic markets, security, environmental sustainability, order and justice. Many people's lives run across state borders, and furthermore, what happens in one place affects what happens in other places, with politics, society, economics, culture and security all becoming cross-border processes. China's rise to global economic and political power provides an illustration of this.

China's economic rise from the 1990s to the present has been partly due to strong Japanese, European and American demand for cheap manufactured products. Stated differently, maintaining the high standard of living in Japan and Europe and North America has been partly dependent on cheap Chinese labor supporting China's transformation into the factory of the world. On the minus side for these rich countries, however, this inflow of cheaper Chinese imports caused a decline in domestic manufacturing industries and major corporate restructuring.

Looking at the Chinese side of things, the successful expansion of Chinese manufacturing raised living standards especially in the cities, with rising salaries, rising housing costs, and higher standards of living generally. In fact, China has been so successful that labor shortages, combined with higher worker expectations, have caused a rise in the cost of labor there. As a result, manufacturing companies are now shifting their factories to other countries in Asia to lower production costs. In response, the Chinese government is promoting the development of more profitable and high-wage tertiary and quaternary industries to rival the rich advanced countries of the world.

Alongside these fast-shifting economic relationships, however, there are signs of political and social friction. China has expanded its military capabilities to a level that it considers more suitable for its new position as a major player in world affairs. The necessary economic foundation for its military expansion is provided by its profitable trade relations, notably with the United States and Japan. But seeing this military expansion as a threat, Japan's government has shown renewed interest in strengthening its own position. To this end, it is reinforcing its alliance with the United States. It also shows signs of wanting to reinterpret the Constitution to allow more overseas action by the Self-Defense Forces. At the same time, it has also changed the rules on foreign arms sales and arms development, and is increasing the budget for military matters.

Japan has generally welcomed China's economic development. However, it seems unwilling to accept the changes in the Asia-Pacific military balance sought by this wealthier China.

From the perspective of social relations, in the context of Japan's economic and demographic decline and its increasing interdependence with China, anti-Chinese prejudice is visible in public demonstrations, right-leaning weekly magazines, and in discussions on internet forums. Matching such expressions of cultural nationalism in Japan, we can see similar kinds of cultural nationalism in China, where anti-Japanese demonstrations, publications, and official speeches are commonplace.

On a brighter note, student exchanges between the two countries, as well as tourist travel between the two countries, are running at very high levels, and Japanese popular culture is widely consumed in East Asia, including China. While Chinese dramas and music have not yet broken into the Japanese market in any meaningful way, they may yet follow the recent Korean example. Mainland Chinese music and visual media products may, over the next few decades, break into the Japanese market, and help in the gradual creation of a shared East Asian culture sphere.

Overall, some of these major contemporary trends suggest closer integration is happening. Others point to continuing opposition and conflict.

How we understand and respond to these trends goes beyond the responsibility of governments and diplomats and bureaucrats working for international organizations. It calls for the informed involvement of each and every one of us, as consumers of goods and services, as workers who need jobs to survive in market economies, as citizens affected by government policies ranging from security and health and education, as participants in cross-border social relationships and living cultures. This is why, quite simply, everyone needs to be familiar with the fundamental principles of the academic discipline of international relations.

1-1 Change and continuity: perspectives on the past, present, and future

Human beings tend to notice rapid and large-scale change much more than we notice continuity or small-scale gradual change. If a friend changes their hairstyle or fashion, this will make a much greater impression on us than the many ways in which they stay the same. Elements such as hair color, bone structure, body type and so on will attract little attention so long as they appear to be largely the same.

Similarly, if you were able to time-travel thirty years into the past, or thirty years into the future, it is likely that the first things you notice would be the new technologies, the unfamiliar objects, the different social norms. And yet surely there would be just as many things that stay more less the same, but as a result receive less attention, such as perhaps housing, public transport systems, and the institutions and aims of government.

The continuities are just as important as the differences or the things that are new, but are often given less attention, simply because human attention is more easily drawn to differences and to novelty. Being aware of this bias in human perception may help us to begin thinking about the world. That is, when we seek to understand what is going on, we should be careful to look not just at the things that seem to be new, but also at the many examples of continuity.

How might this perspective be useful in thinking about world affairs? If we look at today's world, and compare it to the world of a hundred years ago, then from the perspective of continuity, we might notice that the states of Western Europe and North America still enjoy relatively dominant positions in the world, in terms of economic, political, social, cultural, and military power. We may observe that most of the poor countries of a century ago are still quite poor.

From the perspective of change, however, it is notable that some East Asian countries have joined the ranks of the world's developed countries. We could argue that the Western European and North American advanced states enjoy far less power in the world than they used to, because of decolonization and the increased influence of other countries. We might also add that world politics is becoming more and more globally interconnected, as shown by the dramatic increase in communication, trade and travel between countries, and that a great number of international organizations have been created to help manage the increase in cross-border relations.

From this very simple exercise, we could propose that a major continuity visible over the last century is the fact that a global hierarchy still exists, with the position of each state determined by its political, military and economic power. The positions of some individual states within this hierarchy have changed, but generally, those in privileged positions have maintained their position.

A major difference appears in the fact that the world is becoming much more closely integrated, at least as measured by the increase in cross-border economic, social, cultural and political connections. By considering the world from these two perspectives, we can try to balance our bias towards noticing change more than continuity, and to consider not just how and why things change, but also how and why things stay the same. This understanding is particularly important as a way of helping us to think about what the future will be like. For while we can be sure than many things will be massively different from the way that they are today, it is also certain that a great many things will be quite similar to the way that they are today.

Japan as an example

Let us introduce one final example to reinforce this insight. Today, Japan seems to be standing at the beginning of a long and serious decline. Its population peaked some years ago and is now falling. The proportion of young people is constantly shrinking to record lows, while the proportion of elderly people is annually reaching new record highs. The economic situation is dire: public debt is huge, industries are short of labor and relocating offshore, and there are few signs that sustainable economic growth will improve the situation in the foreseeable future. Social security and pension systems appear to be heading for collapse. Relations with neighboring countries, while very strong in terms of economic interdependence, are quite bad in terms of politics, and also at the level of everyday life, with racist demonstrations against especially Korean and Chinese people becoming common. This general context is probably quite familiar to young students in Japan: it is the one that they have grown up with.

More unfamiliar to them may be the situation of Japan from the 1960s to the 1980s, when rapid economic growth helped Japan to achieve the status of an economic superpower, when Japanese corporations were buying up significant corporate assets around the world, when Japanese people were consuming massive amounts of high-end luxury goods, and there was serious talk of "Japan as number one" in the world. To students born in the 1990s, this era may seem mythical, unreal.

Still more unfamiliar again may be the Japan of the late 1940s and early 1950s, when it was a country literally in ruins, its physical infrastructure largely destroyed, social institutions in upheaval, and people in need of allied assistance to get by. Going back even further, the Japan of the 1930s and early 1940s, when the military held sway over political decision-making and led the invasion of China and Japan's entry into World War II, is perhaps even more remote from the daily experience of today's students. To set out Japanese modern history in this simplified form makes us focus on huge discontinuities or change. Looking at the situation purely from this perspective, we might think that what the future will bring is massively uncertain.

However, if we take a step back from the differences between the Japanese situation in these different eras, and look for some of the similarities, we may notice that what leaders focus on in the field of national security has remained largely the same. In the Meiji period, the government stressed the need to industrialize and militarize to restore and maintain Japan's sovereignty. It was for national power and security that Japan launched itself into the Sino-Japanese and Russo-Japanese wars, and the colonization of Taiwan and Korea. Similarly, it was to maximize national power and prestige that it invaded China and attacked the United States. In the postwar era, it was to protect national security that a security treaty was signed with the United States, and US bases permitted to remain on Japanese and especially Okinawan soil after independence. Today, in the name of national security, the importance of maintaining the US alliance and of boosting Japanese military power is stressed repeatedly. National security has been the central concern of governments in the modern era.

It seems clear that Japan's modern leaders have considered the world to be an uncertain and dangerous place. They have seen the primary concern of leaders as being national security, which was to be assured independently through military strength, or in alliances with other countries. In this sense, it may be reasonable to predict that things will not be greatly different in the future, and that national leaders will continue to treat national security as their primary concern, and other issues as secondary.

1-2 The three levels of analysis and international relations

Events and situations have causes. Understanding those causes can help us to predict what will happen in the future. The better we are able to understand causes, the better we should be able to predict what lies ahead. One important way of thinking about causes in the field of international relations is to try and separate them out analytically into three levels, or into system, state, and individual level factors.

Briefly, system-level factors are those that are connected to the nature of the international system: the actors, the kinds of power that they possess, and how their relationships with other actors. Knowing what kind of system exists should help in understanding what actors do within that system.

However, system-level explanations can't account for everything. We should also look at state-level factors, or at the particular characteristics of individual countries, because they are likely to affect what states do. For example, whether a state is democratic or authoritarian, rich or poor, Christian or Buddhist, militaristic or pacifistic, a former empire or a former colony, are all likely to have different effects on the policies and relationships of that state. Knowing the particular nature of each state should help in understanding the policies and relationships of that state.

Of course, even though we might talk about states as though they are united actors, it is also true that in the end, it is particular people who make actual policy, and take actual action. Thus understanding international relations also calls on us to think about the

13

individual level of analysis, and about what people are like as individual members of a species, and as members of groups in society.

The end of the Cold War: an example

The end of the Cold War provides us with an example of how this set of tools can help us to understand events. Many students may remember the leaders of the USSR and the USA at the time were Mikhail Gorbachev and Ronald Reagan respectively, and consider that these two played a key role in ending the conflict between the two superpowers. In particular, they may say that the strong anti-Soviet position taken by a resolute Reagan forced the pragmatist Gorbachev to accept that the decline of the USSR would no longer allow it to keep its empire under control. Such an explanation would tend to focus on how individual-level factors—determination, strength of resolve, pragmatism and so on—affected the actions of leaders, and how those actions changed the world. This may be true. However, we need also to remember that the actions of individuals take place in a larger context, such as the domestic situation in the state where they operate.

In the case of the Soviet Union, for example, a severe economic decline had been occurring, leading to an ever-deepening gap in living standards with the capitalist world. Further, as the economic situation deteriorated, people in the peripheral Soviet states, as well as in the core states of the USSR, were increasingly unhappy with their lives. New media allowed them to see living conditions elsewhere, and aroused in them a desire for change. Political unrest and rising nationalism were major problems for those who wished to hold the Soviet Union together. If Gorbachev was pragmatic, it was perhaps because circumstances did not allow him to be anything else. And if Reagan took a hard line against the Soviets, it was because the US was economically and militarily much more powerful that the USSR, and enabled him to do so. The fact that the USA had a much stronger position than its opponent made it possible for Reagan to be strong and resolute. In this sense, individual level factors were determined by state-level conditions.

However, considering the end of the Cold War in terms of individual and state level factors does not yet give us a full picture. We need to add the systemic level or the global conditions in which the USSR and the USA existed, in order to think about the overall context in which the Cold War ended. In global terms, capitalism appeared to be much more successful than communism in achieving material prosperity, as shown by the economic rise of US allies such as Japan and Korea. Also, the United States' model of a society that valued individual freedom and rights, especially as it was symbolized in a wide range of film, television and music products that were consumed around the world, allowed it to be much more successful in attracting allies. By comparison, the Eastern bloc had suffered economic stagnation, did not present an attractive social model except in state propaganda, produced few popular cultural products, and was far behind the Western bloc countries in terms of economic, military, and also cultural power. The simple fact of Western dominance, and the dire situation of the Eastern side, suggested that the end of the Cold War was inevitable. Rather than being a remarkable and sudden development, it was the logical consequence of long-term trends in the global distribution of economic, financial, social, cultural, and military resources.

In review, we can suggest that in order to understand why the Cold War ended, it is important to consider how factors at the three levels of analysis fit together. While the system determines the overall field of what is possible or likely and impossible or unlikely, each state's characteristics affect the way in which particular events take place. Similarly, the individual characteristics of leaders may also make a difference. However, it may be possible to argue that the individual level factors are less important than the state and system level factors, given than the actions individuals can take are strongly determined by the larger state and systemic contexts in which they find themselves. This point becomes clearer when we look at the different types of causes in terms of how close or far they are in time from the effects that they are related to, or at proximate and underlying causes.

1-3 Proximate and underlying causes

What does it mean to say that X caused Y? We can answer this question with reference to our example above in several different ways. To say that Reagan's determination or Gorbachev's pragmatism caused the end of the Cold War would be to talk about how proximate causes at the individual level of analysis caused the Cold War to end at a particular moment, in a particular way. But we might also consider the following question. Why was this event—in this case the end of the

Cold War—asking to happen?

In other words, what were the long-term roots of the situation that made the end of the Cold War likely, that made it possible for Gorbachev and Reagan to put an end to the Cold War? To answer this, we would have to go back further in time, to look at state and system-level factors such as the relative difference in the efficiencies of capitalist and communist economies, or differences in the attractiveness of the respective ideologies and societies, and so on. This would be a more difficult question to answer, but it would be more significant, in that it tells us more about what we should do, or what we should avoid doing. This can be made clear by looking at a few examples from everyday life.

Take the case of the driver of a car who was badly injured when he crashed and was thrown through the windshield. In this case, the proximate cause of his injury is the fact that he was thrown through the windshield. In this case, the lesson we could take is that it is good to avoid being thrown through windshields. But this is a fairly meaningless kind of recommendation.

If, however, we consider the underlying or remote cause of the driver's injury, we might say that it occurred because he wasn't wearing a seat-belt, and so was thrown through the windshield when he crashed. In this case, an analysis of the underlying cause of the driver's death points to the recommendation—from the viewpoint that it is good to reduce deaths on the road—that it is important to use seat belts when traveling in a car. This second recommendation is much more meaningful than our first.

Proximate and remote causes of World War

To take a few more examples, consider that the proximate cause of World War I may be said to be the assassination of the Austrian Arch-Duke Franz Ferdinand. But knowing this doesn't really provide us with any great insights, or lead to significant policy recommendations. Saying that it is desirable to prevent the assassination of important figures is nothing more than stating the obvious. On the other hand, if we look at underlying causes, then we might talk about how a system of competing alliances led to an escalation of tension, and of how the military capabilities of the time gave a decisive advantage to whoever was the first to attack. These factors provided European states of the time with an incentive to seek excuses to launch military action.

Considering these kinds of system-level underlying causes would encourage us to recommend, in the interests of peace, that universal collective security arrangements are more desirable than competing alliances, and that it is desirable to establish security arrangements which do not advantage whoever is the first to attack.

In the case of World War II, the proximate causes may again be identified at an individual level in the actions of Adolf Hitler. His personality and beliefs, as revealed in his decision-making, led to the establishment of fascist rule in Germany, as well as to the invasion of Poland, and to conflict all around the world. But to find the proximate cause of the Second World War in the fact that a charismatic but aggressive leader came to power does not provide any particularly deep insights. The recommendation that we should avoid letting charismatic leaders with aggressive personalities attaining powerful positions is so superficial that it is hardly worth making.

If we look, rather, at the underlying causes that allowed someone like Hitler to come to power, and to make the kinds of decisions that he did, and to put them into practice, we would have to consider factors such as the great resentment in Germany over the settlement to the first world war, and in particular the punitive conditions of the Treaty of Versailles. Our attention would also be drawn to the problem of economic nationalism and protectionist policies that cause downturns in international trade, and so intensify global economic depressions. We would also have to consider the shortcomings of collective security under the newly established League of Nations, and the inability of international law in the form of the Kellogg-Briand Pact to prevent aggressive war.

Consideration of these state and system-level underlying causes of World War II would lead us, perhaps, to the recommendation that victors in war should take steps to make a system that reintegrates the losers in the postwar international order. In fact, the allied treatment of Germany and Japan after World War II suggests that this was well-understood by leaders of the time. Secondly, it would also lead us to a deeper understanding of the utility of free trade in enhancing the possibility of international peace. Lastly, it might also lead us to the position that collective security arrangements should be not only universal, but also have mechanisms and institutions capable of enforcing punitive sanctions against states that violate international law.

17

To review this section, we note that system, state and individual level causes of events and decisions can be positioned in a time sequence, based on how close they are in time to the event or decision. The most proximate causes are often the best-known, especially in cases where they involve the decisions and actions of individuals. But looking at the bigger picture, proximate causes appear less interesting than the underlying factors that make an event possible or even likely. Understanding the underlying factors of events can make it possible to think about ways to promote desirable events, or prevent undesirable events. This is usually more meaningful than thinking about ways to prevent or promote particular individual-level proximate causes.

1-4 Academic investigation and the problem of perception

Grasping world affairs in an academic manner involves understanding events and trends. It should include the identification of patterns in these events and trends, which can allow students to make generalizations and explanatory theories based on these patterns. To do these things, we might investigate historical data, examine statistics, or observe real-world interactions between different kinds of international actors. This introductory chapter has so far looked at how the concepts of change and continuity, as well as tools such as the three levels of analysis, and consideration of proximate and underlying causes, can help us out in these tasks. But next, before we go on to look at key theoretical frameworks of the academic discipline of international relations, it is necessary to review some psychological characteristics common in human beings that can make rational and open-minded consideration of world affairs different.

Dealing with the issue of human bias is one of the more difficult problems that we face in doing scientific analysis. Although we may pretend to be rational and objective in our thinking and decision-making, in reality, we are often unsuccessful. Often, we engage in sloppy thinking using simplistic mental maps, make decisions based on prejudices and stereotypes, and generally suffer from a range of cognitive biases. In this section, we outline a few of these, to show what we mean, and also to emphasize how important theories and concepts are in trying to overcome these biases. In particular, we will look at the concepts of mental maps, confirmation bias, cognitive dissonance, and schematic reasoning.

Chapter 1 Social Science and International Relations

Maps and mental maps

Some of our biases come from culture, from the way that information is transmitted to us. For example, any political map of today's world, showing around two hundred states, suggests to us that it is normal for the world to be divided into many sovereign states. But if we look at the world from space, then we get a sense that political borders are insignificant, compared to the geographical, environmental and climatological unity of the world. Such political maps, in other words, may work to limit our thinking—we may accept the current political divisions as natural, whereas they are the result of historical processes—and discourage us from alternative ways of thinking about a different kind of world.

Figure 1 Mercator projection

To continue with the theme of maps a little further, it is obvious that turning a roughly spherical and three-dimensional earth into a rectangular two dimensional map is problematic. However, despite the biases that are unavoidable in maps, we still rely on them. This is because they give us a simplified representation of the world, which can help us in our understanding. For example, the Mercator projection accurately shows countries' shape, as well as the distance between locations. Historically, this type of map was of great value to travelers. However, it distorted the size of countries, making Eurasian and North

19

American countries much too large compared to China, Africa, India, and other southern countries. This led to complaints that the map presented a bias in favor of the world's rich and powerful countries in the so-called north, and against the weaker developing countries of the so-called south.

One response to such criticism was the Peters projection, which shows the relative sizes of the continents correctly. By doing this, Peters tried to produce a map that showed the world's countries in the proper proportion to each other. However this map too, is not without its problems. Especially, it tends to have a vertically stretched feel. No map, in fact, is without its own particular issues, and we must remind ourselves that our maps are, in the end, a matter of convention and convenience rather than an objective representation of how the world is.

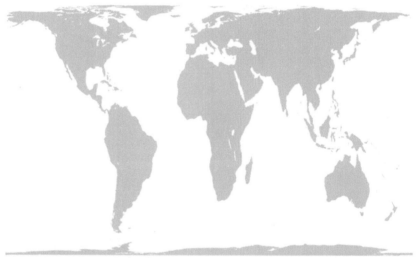

Figure 2 Peter's Projection

Maps simplify existing reality, adapting it into a form that is useful or informative. But we need to be careful that such shortcuts to understanding do not lead us away from knowledge.

That is, we need to be aware that our understandings are often based on mental maps: beliefs about what the world is like, what is true and what is false, reasonable and unreasonable. We acquire these beliefs in everyday life from a wide range of sources, including friends, family, media, books, and teachers. The problem is that not only is our understanding often imperfect, the understanding of others too, is frequently mistaken. Thus our mental maps include lots of untested and wrong ideas. Holding mistaken beliefs is not a huge problem if we are willing to constantly test and update our ideas. But this is rarely the case.

Confirmation bias

It is well known in psychology that once people develop strongly held beliefs, they dislike questioning those beliefs. In fact, many experiments show that people will actively look for evidence that supports their beliefs, but show little attention to information and ideas that do not. In some advanced economies, such as the United States, many people believe that anybody can be successful in economic, political and social life, as long as they are happy to make great efforts and sacrifices. Statistically, of course, being born into an upper-middle class family makes it relatively easy to succeed, whereas being from a poor working class family makes it hard to succeed. But this belief in all individuals sharing an equal chance of success is so popular that people pay great attention to those who overcome great obstacles to become leaders in a particular field, and tend to ignore the fact that the vast majority of people experience little social mobility. That is, believing that a society offers all members equal opportunities leads people to focus on cases that support this view, and to pay little attention to cases that deny it.

This kind of tendency appears in international relations too, as people acquire fixed beliefs about certain states as being good or friendly, and other states as being bad or unfriendly. This leads them to focus on evidence that supports these ideas, and to ignore evidence that suggests a different version of reality. In Japan, examples of this can be found in the beliefs that North Korea is bad and untrustworthy, whereas the United States is good and trustworthy. Such beliefs lead people to be interested in proof of North Korean misdeeds and American benevolence. Conversely, it makes them less interested in evidence that suggests the possibility of North Korean change for the better, or examples of illegal or ethically dubious American actions around the world. Thus people's view of international relations is filtered by what they already believe about the world. The consequence is that people pay attention to events that support and reinforce their position. This tendency is known as confirmation bias.

Cognitive dissonance

Closely connected with this phenomenon is cognitive dissonance. This refers to a situation in which a contradiction arises between what a person believes, and what they actually do. A common example given to explain this concept is that of the smoker who knows that smoking is bad for people's health. In such a case, assuming that the person thinks that health is a good and desirable thing, there is a tension between the act of smoking and the knowledge that smoking has negative effects on various organs of the body. Psychologically, such a contradiction produces stress, and people then look for ways to resolve the dissonance this stress causes.

The smoker has several options to resolve this tension. The most obvious is to stop smoking, so that action and belief become consonant. But in many cases, this appears to be difficult. Cigarettes contain the drug nicotine, which is addictive, and many smokers become physically dependent. Instead, smokers may seek to resolve the conflict in a way that allows them to keep on smoking. They may say something like, "Smoking is said to be bad for people's health, but my grandfather and father both smoke, and they are very healthy and happy". Alternatively, they may claim that it is better to enjoy life and cigarettes, even if they die earlier than they otherwise would. In this case, they would be claiming that a longer life without cigarettes is worth less than a shorter life with cigarettes. Other possibilities include rejecting the claim that cigarettes are harmful altogether by saying that the science is uncertain, or that the evidence is not yet sufficient. The stress produced by cognitive dissonance is often resolved like this, in ways that allow the original belief or desire to be upheld and the inconvenient facts to be ignored or dismissed.

In the international relations context, cognitive dissonance may occur when, for example, a country like Japan, whose people are strongly in favor of a world without nuclear weapons according to most opinion surveys, is in reality defended by the United States of America, a superpower that possesses a great number of nuclear arms. The belief that nuclear weapons are evil exists in contradiction with the fact of Japan's security dependence on the United States nuclear umbrella. This tension could be resolved through changing one's thinking on nuclear weapons, or by giving up the alliance with the United States. Both of these, it is clear, would be difficult choices. Alternatively, the tension might be resolved by trying not to think about the dependence on the United States, by claiming that despite possessing them, the United States would never again use nuclear weapons in a war, or by claiming that the grave security threats in East Asia make U.S. nuclear deterrence necessary. In such ways, it might be possible to reconcile the contradiction and relieve tension in a way that allows existing beliefs to be reconciled with a conflicting reality without having to make major changes to either belief or reality.

Attribution bias

Attribution bias is another psychological mechanism that might come into play in this kind of situation. This happens when we consider an action that "we" or "our side" commits in a different way to the same action when it is committed by others, or the "other side". For example, consider that you are late for an important job interview because of a traffic jam. Once the traffic jam clears, you drive at a speed that is well over the limit, telling yourself that the situation justifies your fast driving. But if you see another car drive past you at high speed the next day, you are less likely to be so tolerant. Indeed, rather than wonder what emergency is pushing them to drive at such high speed, you are likely to think of that person as a reckless and thoughtless human being. Attribution bias says that because we tend to know more about our own situation, we can see how circumstances make us do certain things that are morally or legally hard to justify. But in the case of others, we know much less about why they are doing what they are, and so we tend to explain their actions based on personality, even though circumstances probably affect them in the same way that they affect us.

This kind of bias is apparent in the international context too. North Korea exists in an unfriendly international environment, where regional neighbors such as the Republic of Korea and Japan are much richer, militarily vastly more powerful, and both enjoying the protection of the United States' nuclear arsenal. The United States not only considers North Korea as an enemy state, the U.S. also has a history of overturning by covert or overt means the governments of states that it considers to be unfriendly, such as in the recent cases of Iraq, Afghanistan and Libya. North Korea's sole "ally" is China, which has developed close economic ties to the United States, Korea, and Japan. For the North Korean government, it may be logical, in these circumstances, to develop nuclear weapons capability as a deterrent to American, Korean, Japanese, or even Chinese adventurism, and to protect its national security. And yet the understanding of North Korean nuclear weapons development in other parts of the world often passes over these situational causes of North Korean military programs, and prefers personality-driven explanations that focus on the irrationality or the aggressiveness of the North's leadership (let us be clear here that this is by no means to defend the North Korean regime, which is clearly engaged in massive human rights violations of its own people).

Schematic reasoning

A final phenomenon that we should consider here is known as schematic reasoning (note that this list of psychological biases common in human action is not exhaustive). We engage in schematic reasoning when we use typical patterns or figures that we have encountered in the past in trying to understand new information or events in the present. For example, if you are traveling on the train late at night, and a man smelling strongly of alcohol with a red face and bloodshot eyes dressed in a crumpled suit sits next to you and starts to talk to you, you can probably assume, based on prior first-hand and second-hand experience, that this is a salary-man on his way home from an after-work drinking session, and is likely not very dangerous, even if somewhat obnoxious. If you are shopping for some midnight snacks in a convenience store and some motorcycle-helmet wearing young men come in with knives and shout at the store attendants, you can probably safely assume that you are caught up in the middle of a robbery attempt, based on your secondhand and possibly firsthand experience of robberies, and conclude that you should keep a low profile until the robbers depart.

Using our knowledge of stereotypical situations and people to understand what is unfolding around us and decide how to act can be useful, as in these cases. Patterns and figures based on prior experience give us a framework for evaluating and understanding new situations and people rapidly. Once we make a quick decision about what is going on, or what type of person we are dealing with, we tend to stop trying to consider all the complexities involved. This lets us take quick action without too much thought. However, rapid decisions and actions may not always be so desirable. Our categorization may be off-target, or even completely wrong.

The problem is that we often don't know the precise nature of things, or make mistaken assumptions. Each situation is literally unique, and while past experience may indeed provide a rough guide to what we should do, it can only be a rough guide. Action based on categorization that is overly simplistic can go seriously wrong. Foreign media like to characterize North Korea and North Korean leaders as stereotypical bad guys. Evil, obsessed with weapons, drugs and sex, they are basically represented the same way as the cartoon-like bad guys in James Bond movies. Such characters are to be assassinated, not negotiated with seriously. If we follow this kind of stereotyped thinking, then negotiation and cooperation with the North Korean leadership becomes unimaginable.

However, in reality, diplomats and bureaucrats with first-hand knowledge of North Korea talk about how the North has a highly rational leadership, which is playing a high-stakes game involving the nuclear card to win concessions and aid from other countries, at least partly because it considers that the USA has not fulfilled past promises of cooperation and assistance (Obviously, the US position is that the North has not met the conditions to receive cooperation and assistance). The cartoon-like image of the North as an evil state thus becomes a serious problem in terms of dealing with and improving the actual situation regarding North Korea.

A whole range of psychological tendencies thus can operate to limit rational and objective thinking and decision-making by human beings. Favoring our own beliefs and our own ideas over real evidence, privileging our view of things over that of others, denying or explaining away inconvenient facts and situations, and making decisions based on stereotypes are all tendencies that we should avoid. To some extent, just being aware of these pitfalls will help us. Using the perspectives of change and continuity, the three levels of analysis, and time scales for proximate and underlying causes should also fix or at least somewhat reduce the influence of these biases. We receive further assistance from theories about world politics and international relations, which are discussed in the following chapters.

N.M.

Questions

1. Using one real-world example, discuss the advantages and disadvantages of explaining an event in international relations from each of the three levels of analysis.

2. Using one real-world example, explain the differences between remote and proximate causes of an event in international relations.

3. How has the world changed over the last 100 years? How has it stayed the same? Compare and contrast today's world with the world of 100 years ago, focusing on the actors, their aims, and their capabilities.

4. Explain, using examples, why we need to be careful about perception when studying international relations?

5. Choose one of the following, and explain what it means, using examples from your life as well as world politics. Confirmation bias, Cognitive dissonance, Attribution bias, Schematic reasoning

Chapter 2: The modern interstate system

"At bottom, every state regards another as a gang of robbers who will fall upon it as soon as there is an opportunity." Schopenhauer

Although the world has never had as many sovereign states as it does today, increasing cross-border exchanges in our age of globalization are strengthening the idea that we live in one world. Here, we examine the historical development and spread of the inter-state system. In looking at its success, we also wish to draw attention to the possibility of its end.

The modern state can be defined as a territory with a resident population, clearly defined and internationally recognized borders, and a government that has ultimate power over what happens within that territory.

This last point is perhaps the most important characteristic of modern states: they are considered to be sovereign. That is, their governments have ultimate authority over all domestic economic, financial, political, social, and cultural matters. All internal actors, such as religions, companies, local governments, universities and so on stand beneath the government of the state they exist within, and cannot legitimately reject or ignore its orders.

Similarly, external actors such as other states, intergovernmental organizations, and non-governmental organizations have no legitimate power over the domestic actions of a government. What a government does inside its borders is its own business, and not that of any other state. Interference in the domestic affairs of another state is forbidden, at least in principle.

Enjoying all of these rights depends, of course, on gaining international recognition as a state, which is why diplomacy is very important. Once recognized as a state by other states, all states are supposed to possess sovereignty equally, regardless of their size or power. This leads, of course, to the principle mentioned above, that no state should violate the international boundaries of another. Thus the government of a state has ultimate authority over domestic matters, and is at the same time obliged not to violate the sovereignty of other states.

These principles can be understood as international rules that are designed to help prevent warfare and armed conflict in the world. Firstly, if states are not allowed to violate the sovereignty of other states, then the incidence of war between states should decline, or even fall to zero, so long as states follow this rule. Also, if governments of states hold sovereign power over all domestic actors, then internal peace too, should be achievable. Civil war, local armed conflict, guerrilla fighting and so on should all be eliminated, as state governments establish a monopoly on the use of legitimate violence within a state.

2-1 The Treaty of Westphalia

These rules concerning sovereignty were created in Western Europe as part of the Treaty of Westphalia, which brought an end to the Thirty Years War in 1648. On one level, this war involved a struggle between Catholicism and Protestantism, or between the established Church, which emphasized that Catholic institutions should interpret the Bible and guide believers as to what Christ believed, and a new Church emphasizing that people should read the Bible for themselves and have a more individual relationship with God. Catholic and Protestant forces fought for their own positions, and against the right of others to hold different beliefs about Christianity. However, religion was hardly the only reason for the Thirty Years War continuing on for such a long time. Another major issue was the fact that many local lords possessed their own private armies, liked fighting because of the profits they could obtain from war booty, and were not under the control of their head of state. Rulers' power and authority was not always strong enough to stop such warlords from going to war.

At the peace conference held in the Westphalian cities of Munster and Osnabruck, representatives of the many warring parties negotiated and signed an agreement to bring about a "Christian and Universal Peace, and a perpetual, true, and sincere Amity" to end three decades of fighting and destruction. The signing parties promised that states and their rulers were to govern their territories as they saw fit in terms of laws, taxation, war, diplomacy, and religion, without the interference of any other party, for any reason. Disputes over the form of government inside a country, whether monarchical, republican, or constitutional monarchist, were to be settled by the central state, as were debates concerning the position of particular religions within a country. Warlords and religious leaders both would come under the authority of the central state, which would be able to act in the knowledge that outside forces—religious groups, warlords, states— were not allowed to get involved in internal struggles. Politics and religion within a state were no longer to lead to international war, and domestic war should be eliminated by the state, with its new monopoly over the legitimate use of force.

2-2 The centralization of power

After the sovereign state system emerged in Western Europe, it gradually spread to other parts of the world. The global expansion of the modern state system must be explained with reference to a range of economic and political developments. One is the fact that sovereignty gave governments of states much greater power.

Modern states provide their citizens with five major things of value: security and freedom through military-backed independence in the world, order and justice through domestic governance and responsible participation in international institutions and by following international norms, and citizen welfare through economic policies including redistribution. The state plays a remarkably large role in our daily lives, although we generally only pay attention to it when things go wrong, in emergencies and crises. Prior to the development of this modern state, however, state functions were dispersed among different actors who held different types of power.

Feudal lords and their military vassals were primarily responsible for the maintenance of order. Freedom was limited generally to the ruling classes, while overall order was theoretically the responsibility of kings and emperors, who however rarely had enough effective power to control their entire territories. Justice was partly a religious matter, and partly a matter dealt with by local rulers, while welfare was part of the relationship between feudal lords and their peasants. Generally, lords lived off the economic production of their peasants, but in hard economic times, they were considered to owe their peasants assistance.

Centralization and power

These decentralized patterns of power and responsibility were centralized and coordinated within the sovereign states that constituted the Westphalian interstate system. Whereas feudal lords might once have each had their own army, their own land, their own taxation systems, and even their own separate laws, sovereign governments began to consolidate their power by building unified militaries, centralizing tax collection, making national economic policy, and establishing state-wide law codes.

Having one army instead of many, or one economic policy and market instead of many, for example, meant that compared to the past, societies, politics, and economies were much more integrated, rational and efficient. One effect of this tendency towards centralization was that states were able to enjoy vastly more power, compared to the amount that the various actors had previously enjoyed within the old decentralized states.

Nationalism and power

A further innovation that helped the new states become much stronger than any preceding them was that they came to treat people not as passive objects to be ruled over or dominated, but rather as active agents who could and should participate in matters of government. Fundamentally, this reflected the influence of the ideology of nationalism, which became especially influential after the French Revolution towards the end of the eighteenth century.

During the French Revolution, the revolutionary masses killed the monarch and declared that they were no longer subjects of the king, but rather citizens of a state that belonged to them. Sovereignty should not lie in the king or the royal house, but in the people. Naturally, this meant that the people should engage in government, or at least, that government policies should follow the will and promote the interests of the people, rather than promote the interests of the rulers themselves. The idea that the people of sovereign states formed a community known as a nation, and that this nation held sovereignty over the states where they lived, became one of the most important political ideas of the modern era in at least two ways. From the perspective of ordinary people, this ideology was used to claim greater say in how they would be governed. But it had another important consequence. It helped enable the state to mobilize people's energies for projects such as imperialism, economic development, and war.

The interests of the ruling authorities and the interests of ordinary people had formerly been distinct, if not completely opposed. For example, whether a feudal lord prospered or not meant little to the peasants who labored on his land, as all rulers set taxes as high as the peasants could bear. Pre-modern politics fundamentally had very little effect on ordinary people, except in regards to higher taxes or lower taxes. War was significant only as it affected local order, or involved the conscription of local men. Whether one side lost or won was fundamentally a matter of interest only to the ruling class. Japan's rulers worried during the 1850s that the ordinary people might join sides with the European powers pressuring Japan to open up to their trading demands. This was because they perceived, quite accurately, that the Japanese people of the time in no way saw that their fates were tied to those of the Tokugawa state in which they lived.

The ideology of nationalism tried to make people think that their individual fates and the fate of their state were directly connected, and so to bring ordinary people to devote themselves to state causes. This was achieved through means such as national education, which teaches people to be citizens of a particular country whose interests they have a special obligation to defend and advance, as well as through military service and war, in which national unity and devotion are produced through conflict with "enemies", and by national media. All of these institutions help to produce an "imagined community" of national citizens who feel an emotional bond with each other such that they feel pride in the achievements of other citizens on the battlefield, in economic competition, or on the sports field, and feel hurt at injuries received by fellow citizens, and also show a willingness to fight, kill, and die for the sake of the national community.

Modern sovereign states were vastly more powerful than preceding state forms, partly because they engaged in the centralization and rationalization of government institutions. Another major basis of their increased power was the fact that as they developed into nation-states, they became able to draw on the subjective energies of their people for state purposes. This made them vastly more powerful than feudal states, who had to use coercion and force to make ordinary people do the bidding of the ruling strata. A third factor that we need to consider is the economic productivity associated with industrial capitalism, which developed in tandem with the modern interstate system.

2-3 Capitalism and industrialization

Capitalism is an economic ideology proposing that capital, which may take the form of land, workers, factories, money, and so on, should be used to make more capital. It sets no particular upper limit on capital accumulation, and says nothing about human happiness or satisfaction. This belief system proposes no destination for humanity, but only an endless process in which capital should be put to work to increase itself. Capitalist ideology and practice is considered to be a core element that defines the modern world, along with sovereign states and nationalism.

In pre-modern non-settled societies, the idea of an endless process of private wealth accumulation was unimaginable. Wealth was fundamentally public, in that what one person possessed had to be shared with others. Also, because such societies had limited means of storing and transporting goods, and lacked a system of money that could act as a portable store of value through time, the accumulation of possessions or material wealth, as the anthropologist Marshall Sahlins points out, could not become a social goal.

For hunter-gatherers such as Australian Aboriginal groups, gaining food and drink were activities that often required just a few hours a day. Activities including story-telling and the maintenance of perhaps the world's most intricate kinship systems were key elements of their materially poor but culture-rich lives.

In pastoral societies too, material wealth accumulation was restricted by the need to be mobile, by environmental limits, and by the absence of money. The development of agriculture, and then feudalism, greatly changed this situation.

The spread of agriculture or settled farming perhaps 10,000 years ago let people produce more food, and so allowed populations to grow. Because farming required that people stay in one place, it also encouraged the construction of larger, more permanent homes, which allowed people to store up possessions over time. Agriculture also required people to make important decisions about crops, labor, harvest, and the division of crops and so on, and led to more complex societies with clear hierarchies of power and wealth. Feudal societies, in which peasants worked on the land of territorial lords, were one outcome of the tendency for power and wealth to become more concentrated in agricultural economies.

However, although feudal rulers especially could accumulate great wealth, increases in wealth could only be gradual, achieved through breeding better crops and stock, improving fertilizers and tools, increasing the area of land under production, managing land better, and trading with other regions. In such conditions, the aim of economic activity is to maintain living standards, and people hope for, rather than expect, small improvements in their situation. Farmers hoped, for example, that a good harvest one year would be followed by another equally good harvest the next year, rather than for endless dramatic improvements. Lords and princes too, knew that endless exploitation and increases in tax and profit were impossible, given that production was heavily dependent on natural forces, and hoped for similar levels of revenue each year.

The emergence of capitalism

Capitalist practices and thinking about endless and rapid growth arose in Western Europe from the Renaissance period onwards, following a long period of scientific and technological development. This process was helped by improvements in the circulation of knowledge due to the development of printing presses, as well as improved transport infrastructure and increased travel. The spread of better knowledge accompanied a decline in the influence of religions, and a rise in more scientific and rational thinking and innovation. Transport networks expanded, and increased trade made people materially richer and better-informed. Populations increased, cities expanded. Being better connected by information and transport networks, different regions increasingly specialized in the production of specific commodities, and traded their products with the specialties of other areas. Economic specialization led to increased production and efficiencies of scale, as well as to greater economic interdependence with other regions. As these processes unfolded from the 11th century to the sixteenth, the meaning of people's economic activity shifted in a highly significant way, towards what we can call capitalism.

To describe a typical feudal context, peasants produced their own food, and traded excess production for other goods that they could not provide themselves. Artisans made goods that they could sell or exchange to obtain necessities. Feudal lords and retainers obtained some things directly from the peasants working on their land, and other luxuries and necessities by exchanging those things with others.

As societies became richer, more populous, and more urban, market economies developed, in which it was possible to buy necessities from others, so long as one had money. In the course of this process, power gradually shifted to urban merchants and traders, whose income and profits exceeded the land- or agriculture-based income of kings and lords. The rise of the merchant classes in Tokugawa Japan provides a classic example of this.

All social groups became caught up in market practices. Peasants became oriented towards producing things that they could sell for the greatest amount of profit. Lords and kings too, became to think more about ways to achieve greater income from their land. Merchants and traders became more active in more diverse economic fields, trying to make the most profit possible. In fact, everyone became a kind of trader, trying to make the most profit possible from the capital assets that they possessed in the markets that they had access to. As this happened, societies became covered by market economies, in which people's main concern was how to make as much money as possible, so that they could buy all the things that they wanted.

The effects of industrial capitalism

With the Industrial Revolution beginning first in England in the 17th century and soon spreading around the European continent, and reaching Japan in the late-nineteenth century, profit-seeking capitalists partnered new machine technology with fossil fuel energy. Building on efficiencies associated not just with specialization but also with a more sophisticated division of labor, modern industrialized factories achieved a massive increase in production capacities.

Production levels were affected by a few limits, however. Firstly, increased production required a greater supply of raw materials to use in the production process. Secondly, the productivity of machines running on fossil fuels was so high that although there were more and more workers employed in manufacturing who earned wages that allowed them a relatively high level of consumption, domestic markets rapidly became saturated all the same, at least in the case of relatively long-lasting or durable consumer goods. In order to maintain production levels and stay profitable, it frequently became necessary to find new markets outside domestic borders.

Within Western Europe, competitive industrialization and protectionism by states eager to maximize their own profits limited the possibilities for expansion. The European states in the modern era were not able to dominate each other, forming alliances to prevent hegemony by any single power. For example, France and Sweden allied against the Hapsburg Empire, then England and Holland joined together against France. Subsequently, Britain, Russia, Prussia and Austria joined forces against Napoleon's France, and then the Concert of Vienna, in which the European powers cooperated to maintain a roughly stable balance of power lasted from around 1815 to 1914. But although they could not dominate each other, the European powers were able to dominate all other areas of the globe. Using their economic, technological, military and organizational superiority, the advanced centralized sovereign states of the modern world system turned to imperialism, and established political control over foreign territories. This was a way of meeting the needs and requirements of industrial production.

Advanced states competed to acquire colonies not just for prestige, but also to obtain raw materials, and markets for their finished goods. They were able to do this in non-European regions of the world because the military, political and administrative power of centralized industrializing nation-states vastly exceeded that of other existing political systems. This gap in power between advanced European states and the rest of the world saw most of Africa, Asia, the Middle East, and Oceania come under some form of European control or domination by the end of the nineteenth century. The Americas, colonized in an earlier wave of mercantilist imperialism from the fifteenth century on, had for the most part already won independence by this time, and had become covered by sovereign states. The Age of Imperialism came to an end for other regions of the world more slowly, accelerating especially after the Second World War.

To sum up, the power of centralized sovereign nation-states was supported by, at the same time that it supported, capitalist industrialization. Capitalist industrialization encouraged imperialism, which sovereign state power enabled. Further, imperialism introduced the rest of the world to capitalist industrialization, as well as to the sovereign state, and to nationalism.

Seeing the power of the sovereign capitalist nation-state, countries such as Japan that were not yet part of the European sovereign state system tried to adapt by creating a centralized state under a new Meiji government, and enacting a wide range of reforms that aimed at achieving recognition of Japan by the Western powers as a sovereign state. This project involved a massive government-driven push for industrialization, military expansion, and nationalism.

Even in other regions of the world that were unsuccessful in avoiding long-term Western domination, the path to independence, without exception, was illuminated by the torch of nationalism, and resulted in the formation of sovereign nation-states that sought—sometimes successfully—to achieve capitalist industrialization. This is, very briefly, how we arrived at the world we have today, of sovereign nation-states in a capitalist global economy.

N.M.

Chapter 2: The modern interstate system

Questions

1. *Explain why the world is covered in states.*
2. *Explain the main functions of the state.*
3. *In what ways are all states the same? What are key ways in which they are different?*
4. *Are there other realistic ways to achieve the functions of the state?*
5. *Explain the significance of the Peace of Westphalia.*
6. *If the modern state is a recent invention, then how likely do you think it is to continue to exist in its current form? Explain your answer with reference to real-world examples.*

Chapter 3 International Relations: history and theory

"If you don't know history, then you don't know anything. You are a leaf that doesn't know it is part of a tree." Michael Crichton

A theory, simply put, is an explanation of how something works. Theories are developed most often through observation and / or logical reasoning. For example, the biological theory of evolution says that animal species evolve in interaction with their environments, becoming better adapted to the conditions in which they live over time. The sociological theory of broken windows says that crime rates are higher in neighborhoods that look neglected and uncared for, and lower in neighborhoods that look like their residents take care of their properties and streets, because people will think that deviant behavior is more likely to be acceptable in run-down areas than well-kept areas. In psychology, relative deprivation theory suggests that a group of people who feel that they lack something that they have a right to, and which other groups around them enjoy, are likely to take steps to change the status quo. Each of these theories was developed by taking observations about living organisms, criminal tendencies, or social movements, and using logic to create a general explanation about why something happens, or why something is the way that it is. In our everyday lives, theories provide the lenses through which we view other people and ourselves; they are the frameworks with which we understand society, and decide how to act. Three examples will help to confirm this point.

3-1 Theory in everyday life

If we walk down a dark and lonely street late at night and encounter a group of drunken strangers who are men, we may feel some anxiety for our safety. But if the drunken strangers are women, then we may feel little or even no anxiety. In those situations, we would be acting according to a theory of society, based on personal and second-hand knowledge, that says drunken people are more likely to be violent than sober people, and that drunken men are far more likely to be violent than drunken women. This theory would recommend we take

Chapter 3 International Relations: history and theory

greater caution in passing by the group of men compared to the group of women.

Supermarkets often place milk, eggs and other popular items in different corners of the store, far away from the entry. Shop managers are trying to make customers move around the store and see many other items as they look for basic necessities. They are working on the theory, developed from observing shoppers and reasoning about buying patterns, that the more different things customers see, the more they will find things they want. The more things customers buy, of course, the better for the store!

Foreign people living in Japan are often happy to leave their luggage unattended for a few moments at train stations and airports, even if they would never do the same in their home countries. They are working from a theory, based on experience and statistics and media messages, that says Japan is remarkably safe and crime-free, at least as compared to many other countries in the world. Viewing life in Japan in this way, they feel that it is not necessary to take great caution in looking after their possessions in public places.

Just as we rely on a wide range of theories about people and society in our everyday lives, we must also use a range of theories in studying international relations. Learning about how the world works or how actors interact on the international stage is a hugely complex undertaking. Actors include non-governmental organizations and inter-governmental organizations, small states and hegemonic states, multinational corporations and world religions, travelers and students, leaders and ethnic groups. Different types of actors have access to different kinds of power. They also have different identities, aims and values. The possibility that one single elegant theory might explain what all actors do in all types of situations seems very small.

Therefore, a range of theoretical approaches are often used in trying to explain cross-border interactions. Because theories about international relations, like those that we use in our everyday lives, are based on observation, experience, and reasoning, and because people's environment and perception differ widely, no theory is accepted as universally valid, or always true. Unlike in natural or physical sciences, there is a lot more disagreement in social science concerning the question firstly of what phenomena are significant—what kinds of things we should be interested in—and secondly of how to interpret and

39

explain those phenomena, or what those things mean. An examination of the international relations theories of realism and liberalism, in terms both of historical development and of the differences in the basic assumptions that they make about the world and about people, provides us with some good examples of this.

3-2 Liberal idealism in the early-twentieth century

Around ten million soldiers killed each other in the First World War, which lasted from 1914 to 1918. Roughly another twenty million soldiers were injured. Soldiers also killed millions of civilians. However, there were few gains, whether in terms of territory, other material benefits, or improved security, for the states that participated in the fighting. Looking back at the war, many people felt that it had all been a terrible waste of life and resources.

How had so many European countries become engaged in such a prolonged and useless war? One important underlying cause was the fact that European countries, over the previous century, engaged in power-balancing: forming and re-forming alliances with different partners to prevent any single state rising to a dominant position. At the time of World War I, the main alliances were between France, Russia and England, or the Triple Entente, and Germany, Austria-Hungary and Italy, or the Triple Alliance. Members of these alliances had security arrangements with other states too, for example, Serbia with Russia, and Belgium with England.

On the one hand, the Triple Entente countries were worried about the rising power of Germany. As for Germany, it was concerned by the efforts of the Triple Entente to block its rise. At the same time, the Austro-Hungarian Empire was gradually weakening, losing territory to Italy, and it feared losing more territory to Serbia.

In this context, the assassination of Frantz Ferdinand, the crown prince of Austria-Hungary, by a Serbian nationalist, gave Austria an excuse to attack Serbia, and to try and reinforce its own domination over other Balkan regions. However, while Austria-Hungary made sure of German assistance, Serbia was able to call on Russian assistance. Germany wanted to avoid fighting both Russia and France at once, and figured that they could quickly overcome France before fighting Russia, and so attacked France by going through Belgium, which was neutral.

Chapter 3 International Relations: history and theory

This brought England into the war, since Belgium was an ally. The war continued to drag in more countries, with far-off parts of the British Empire such as India, Australia and New Zealand sending many troops on the side of the Entente, along with the United States. On the Alliance side, the Ottoman Empire or Turkey was the main supporting power. The fighting continued without any major breakthroughs on either side for four years, during which little ground was lost or won, and soldiers died at a rate of around 6,000 per day.

Many observers thought that the problem had been the fact that the balance of power system had not been able to avert war. Although alliances were supposed to cancel each other out, they had failed to do so, and had in fact led to the global spread of the war. Further, once war broke out, there had been no good way to stop it from spreading and continuing. A new type of international system needed to be designed, thought influential figures such as Woodrow Wilson, the United States president at the time and a former professor of political science. Wilson proposed some ways to make a more secure and peaceful world in his famous fourteen point plan announced in early 1918.

Wilsonian idealism

Apart from putting an end to secret diplomatic agreements between states so that all actors could make decisions based on actual conditions, Wilson proposed establishing freedom of travel and trade, pushing demilitarization, promoting democracy and self-determination, and creating a general association of states that would mutually guarantee the political independence and territorial integrity of all states. These measures would help humanity move towards a more peaceful, prosperous and democratic world, he thought.

Self-determination would allow colonized peoples inside empires the power to decide how they should be governed. Allowing people to decide who they would be governed by should minimize the chance of violent nationalist conflict. Further, allowing people to decide how they would be governed, in a democratic system, should help to minimize the risk of violent international conflict. This was because war imposed huge burdens on people, in lost lives, injured bodies and minds, and economic damage. Politicians who needed the support of voters could be expected to avoid war, as far as possible. Free travel and trade would lead to more and mutually beneficial cross-border connections, which would help to reduce the risk of war. Finally, the

41

establishment of a new international organization to guarantee peace and security, along with a set of new international laws about how it would work, were presented as key steps in creating a peaceful and secure post-World War I international order.

Wilson's plan was later described as an example of liberal idealism. Liberalism might be summarized as an ideology that says that people, using rational thought, can work together to make the world a better place. Liberals proposed that if the lack of an international organization to maintain peace and security was a problem during World War I, then rational human beings should work together to create such an international organization, which would mediate between states in conflicts and help to establish and maintain international peace and order. States should agree to these kinds of measures, liberals thought, because war was wasteful and non-productive. It stopped trade, and it led to huge human and material costs. Peace was obviously in the interests of all states.

Following this line of argument, in 1920, the League of Nations was created, with France, Great Britain and the Soviet Union as the three Permanent Members on a 15-state governing Council. The League was supposed to assure security collectively firstly by adjudicating in interstate disputes, and secondly by intervening in interstate armed conflict.

Focusing on preventing war, liberals also pointed out that people long ago had decided that private killing was wrong, and made laws against it to make the world safer. Thus they proposed that it should be possible for people similarly to decide that war is wrong, and to make laws against it and make the world a better place. Concretely, in 1928, the so-called Pact of Paris, also known as the Kellogg-Briand treaty after the US Secretary of State and the French Foreign Minister of the time, was established. The official name of this agreement was the "General Treaty for Renunciation of War as an Instrument of National Policy." As its name indicates, it basically banned aggressive war, and required member states to find peaceful ways to resolve conflicts between them. Most countries of the world joined this treaty. Again, liberal thinking about ways to achieve a better world looked to be having a real influence on the world situation. However, this turned out to be quite wrong.

Critics of Wilsonian liberalism often described it as idealist or

Chapter 3 International Relations: history and theory

utopian. They meant that it was a theory that proposed how the world should be, rather than a theory that tried to explain the world as it was. In the eyes of these critics, liberal ideas about how to achieve a more secure and prosperous world paid too little attention to the actual nature of the world, and focused too much on visions of how the world could be, ideally. Although liberal ideals sounded nice in theory, it was uncertain that they could ever be achieved in the real world.

In opposition to the liberal ideas of the post-World War I period, a group of critics who claimed that their ideas were based on how the world was, rather than how the world should be, set out a competing framework for understanding world affairs. Their approach became known as "realism".

3-3 Classical realism in the mid-twentieth century

After the First World War, people had been so tired of the fighting that they followed liberal ideas, at least for a short time, and tried to put them into practice. Governments of almost all major states had agreed to establish the League of Nations or joined it, and most signed up to the Pact of Paris. Some progress was visible, from the liberal point of view. Free trade, democracy, and international peace, however, proved difficult objectives to achieve.

Following the Great Depression beginning in 1930, many countries began competitive devaluations of their currency to promote their own country's exports. They also strengthened protectionist trade policies to discourage imports. Although the aim of individual states was to improve their own economic situation, because many states did the same thing at the same time, they caused the level of world trade to drop rapidly, and deepened the global economic depression.

In some countries, widespread popular discontent with the worsening economic situation was a factor in allowing non-democratic governments to take power. Italy and Spain turned to fascism, Germany to Nazism, and Japan to militarism. Germany and Japan quickly left the League of Nations, while Russia joined in 1934 only to leave in 1940. The United States never joined, and this is considered an important reason for the organization's inability to prevent the occurrence of World War II. Japan invaded China in the 1930s and attacked the United States in 1941, while Germany invaded Poland, divided up much of the Baltic states and surrounding regions between itself and the Soviet Union, and declared war on France and England in 1939.

A world of conflict

Rather than cooperating to make a better, wealthier and safer world as they had promised, states were basically looking out for their own interests. They were willing to use virtually any means possible, including aggressive military force, to do so. The English historian E.H. Carr, in his famous 1939 work, The twenty year's crisis, tried to explain why liberal idealism had failed, and how interstate relations should be understood.

Carr took the position that the liberal vision was all wrong. Liberals had dreamed about the kind of world they would like to live in, and tried to create it. But the idea that people and states could have shared interests in security and economics, and that states could be bound by international law without a higher authority to oversee them was just a fantasy, he thought. It hardly needs to be said that Carr believed it was dangerous to make policy based on fantasy.

Rather than beginning with an ideal and trying to make it come true, Carr proposed that it was important to begin with a proper understanding of the existing reality. And the reality was, he claimed, that there were unavoidable and very deep conflicts of interest between states. For example, there would always be profound conflicts between those states that were developed, prosperous and powerful, and those that were less developed, poorer and weaker. While the well-off states would tend to be satisfied with the existing international system, the others would prefer to try and change the system. This was, for example, a key point in considering the outbreak of World War II, with Germany preferring to modify the status quo, whereas England and France much preferred to keep things as they were. In Carr's view, the study of international relations should focus on the fact that world affairs are fundamentally conflictual. This perspective was described as "realist", in opposition to the liberal "idealist" position.

Self-interested humanity

The work of Hans J. Morgenthau, a German and Swiss educated scholar of international law and international relations who worked mainly in the United States, played a key role in further developing the realist theory of international relations. In his work

Politics among nations, which was first published in 1948, he tried to explain that international relations were unavoidably characterized by conflict and struggle. In his view, this was because humans were naturally self-interested and power-seeking.

Writing in the aftermath of a war in which Germany under Hitler, Italy under Mussolini, and Japan under militarism had aggressively tried to expand their territory, Morgenthau's realism sought to explain liberalism's failure at the individual level of analysis. Basically, just as humans sought power in order to advance their own interests at the individual level, so too did states try to get as much power as possible to advance their own interests in the world. All people have a lust for power, and they like to take advantage of the weaknesses of others. Everyday life, like international relations, was a daily power struggle.

Individual people could enjoy some degree of security against the aggressive actions of others within their states, where they came under the protection of state governments. But this kind of security was not possible in the international system, where states were the highest authority and not under the control of any organization or person. Strong states were sure to try to take advantage of weak states, and to promote their own interests even if they had to harm the interests of others to do so. The international system, because of human self-interest and lust for power, was unavoidably dangerous. In these circumstances, it was vital for states had to take action to protect their citizens against other states.

States bore a special responsibility for the security of their citizens, Morgenthau argued. Looking after their citizens was a primary obligation that was so important that it could not be evaluated using conventional morality. Evil actions, such as violations of foreign citizens' human rights, assassinations of enemy leaders, bombing cities full of foreign civilians and so forth might be necessary evils, required to avoid being conquered by another state. International relations were a tragic affair, in which privately good people might have to engage in these kinds of evil acts in order to protect the safety of people who depended on the state for their security.

The quest for international security

Carr argued that the only way to ensure peace in such an international system made of power-hungry and self-interested states was to engage in balance of power politics. To maximize their chances of survival and autonomy in international relations, states should seek to acquire as much power as possible independently, and when necessary, also form flexible alliances with other states to block hegemonic attempts by other states or alliances. So long as all sides had relatively equal military power in the world, war should be discouraged, because there would be little likelihood of anyone winning decisively or quickly.

In the early years of the Cold War, this view of the world and international relations—based on the concept of a flawed humanity—came to be known as classical realism, and became a dominant framework for understanding world affairs. Humans were claimed to be self-interested and power-seeking, as were the states that humans made. As though exemplifying this in the real world, the United States and the Soviet Union were actually engaged in a struggle for supremacy, forming and re-forming alliances with other states in trying to strengthen their own side's position against the other. Small and medium states that lacked the ability to guarantee their own security independently tended to ally with one of the two superpowers, in an attempt to ensure as much autonomy as possible in a bipolar system.

Life inside states might have become civilized and safe because of the establishment of sovereign state governments, but life among states seemed still to follow the law of the jungle, and security still depended on balance of power politics. The Cold War superpowers' security policies, based on this perception, rested on developing the capability to annihilate not just the other side, but the entire world with nuclear weapons, in their attempt to become powerful enough to deter attack by the other.

From a liberal viewpoint, however, changes in the international situation during the postwar period suggested that classical realism was not able to explain everything that was going on. Although it did not have the material power to oversee state actions, the League of Nations had been re-born as the United Nations, this time with the United States as a key member alongside the Soviet Union, France, Britain and China. Also, the rising level of mutually beneficial cross-border interactions suggested that peaceful cooperation was not an impossible dream. While taking a more cautious approach than the liberal idealists of the post-World War I era, a new group of theorists began to construct what

Chapter 3 International Relations: history and theory

would be known as the neo-liberal theory of international relations.

3-4 Neo-liberalism in the postwar era

During the postwar era, conflict and struggle were not the only major features of relations between states. In fact, from the 1950s onwards, world affairs became increasingly interdependent, in terms of financial and economic issues in particular. The rising levels of cross-border investments and loans, trade, travel and communication suggested that human nature was not as bad as realists feared.

The renaissance of liberal thinking was supported by, for example, European integration, where former enemies began cooperating firstly in strategically important industries, then moving towards trade and investment and long-term cooperation, including political, economic, social, cultural and financial integration. In Asia, the relationship between Japan and the United States shifted 180 degrees, from bitter enemies in war, to a cooperative long-term economic relationship. Liberal thinkers considered that as Western Europe and Japan became wealthy consumer societies, the importance of power politics in an anarchic system was decreasing.

Realism didn't explain these kinds of state action in the emerging international system particularly well, so a new kind of liberalism that was less utopian and more scientific began to be developed, to try and provide a better explanatory framework for what was happening.

Explaining an interconnected world

The main point of neo-liberal theories of international relations was that transformations in domestic politics and in interstate relations were creating a new liberal order, in which cross-border activities centering on trade, finance, and social relations were leading to increased mutual prosperity, as well as shared values and identities. Scholars such as Joseph Nye and Robert Keohane, in their book Power and interdependence (1977) wrote about how transnational interaction was creating a system of complex interdependence linking especially Japan, Western Europe and the United States. In this system, the political agenda of states was less focused on military power, and force was no longer considered a legitimate tool of policy-making.

Modernization and industrialization were the main agents

driving this change. They led to increasing economic specialization, as countries focused on making higher value things that they were comparatively good at. Since countries couldn't specialize in everything, specialization necessarily led to higher levels of cross-border interdependence, as countries traded with other countries to sell their products and to obtain the things that they didn't make themselves.

The keys to greatness in this new world order were no longer territory and natural resources, but rather economic development and trade. Japan and Germany were good examples of this transformation in the nature of power. These two states, which enjoyed low levels of military spending because of security guarantees by the US, had a relatively low level of economic self-sufficiency, and a high level of dependence on other states for trade, both in terms of imports and exports.

Other key neo-liberal insights included the point that the states that were strongly interconnected to each other were often wealthy as a result of their trading relations. Further, they tended also to have democratic governments, and often were deeply involved in international organizations, which of course helped to maintain smooth interstate relations. The neo-liberal argument proposed that trade-based interdependence, political systems oriented towards non-violent conflict resolution, and participation in international organizations were all important factors that discouraged state involvement in armed conflict with other states.

In summary, postwar neo-liberalism focused on how the world was becoming tied together through economic, financial and social connections, and on how these ties, bound up with democracy and trade, seemed to be reducing the risk of war. Further, these trends were supported by an increasingly large and influential number of international organizations, as well as a developing body of international norms and laws. All of this tended to suggest that the world was heading for a more peaceful future. The task of liberal policy-makers and intellectuals, then, was to promote these conditions, namely by encouraging free trade, democratization, and international institutions and organizations around the world.

The fact that the world was in reality becoming more and more interconnected, and that there were obvious cases of cooperation and even deep trust between states, as well as a decline in aggressive actions especially by rich democracies towards other democratic states, meant that neo-liberalism began to gain more and more support as a theoretical perspective useful in understanding the world system, and in designing directions for a safer future world system. The most important critical response to the neo-liberal perspective was termed neo-realism.

3-5 Neo-realist international relations theory

Rather than focusing on economic and social cross-border relations in the postwar world, the leading neo-realist theorist Kenneth Waltz looked at the world from the perspective of how the overall system was structured, and how that structure affected actors inside that system. Fundamentally, he emphasized the fact that the system was made up of sovereign states, and so was in a state of ungoverned anarchy. All states in this system, he observed, had to perform the same tasks: they had to provide security to their citizens, promote economic activity, manage taxation, and so on. All states also shared a basic aim: they wanted to preserve their autonomy and security. But there was one big difference between the states in the system: they all had different amounts of power in the system.

The fact that different state actors had different power capabilities meant that they would tend to follow different patterns of action in their interstate relations. Namely, Waltz argued that great powers would tend to balance each other to stop other great powers from achieving hegemony or global dominance, while smaller weaker states would tend to align with one of the great powers to prevent domination by other great powers and preserve the greatest possible degree of autonomy.

The Cold War context

This particular theoretical framework, which became known as neo-realism in opposition to the earlier classical realism that focused on the individual level of analysis, was based on a system-level examination of security-related matters in the global system during the Cold War. The United States and the Soviet Union were the two superpowers, vastly more powerful than any other state actors. The United States was the only threat to the military security of the Soviet Union, and vice versa. To assure their own security, they both

49

emphasized balancing the power of the other side, through developing their own power capabilities, and making strategic alliances with other states.

Other medium and small states in this system were vastly less powerful than the two superpowers. In response to the problem of how to achieve maximum autonomy in a bipolar global system, many of them chose to align themselves with the United States, as Japan and Korea and Taiwan did, or with the Soviet Union, as in the case of Vietnam, Laos and Cambodia. Only a few states remained completely unaligned.

Cooperation between states did occur in this system, between superpowers and ordinary states, and between ordinary states. However, Waltz said, it was limited.

One factor that limited cooperation was the desire of all state actors to maximize their power and autonomy, and to avoid becoming too dependent on others. Another was the fact that neo-realists saw all states to be fundamentally self-interested. They would follow international agreements and keep promises to others, so long as they perceived it to be in their interests. But there was no guarantee that such a situation would continue indefinitely. To trust in other states was, fundamentally, a risky thing, and so something to be avoided. Finally, the fact that the benefits of cooperation were often unevenly distributed was also a problem for neo-realists. Cooperation might benefit all parties. But this would be meaningless, neo-realists considered, if others gained relatively more benefits.

Neo-realist theory was based on the existing Cold War security situation. It paid little attention to deepening interdependence. Waltz and other neo-realists privileged the political and especially military field, or what some call "high politics", and gave little consideration to other areas such as economics, finance and society, which some call "low politics".

Neo-realists argued that neo-liberals paid insufficient attention to security matters in a system that was still anarchic, despite the massive increase in the number and influence of transnational institutions. In turn, neo-liberals argued that neo-realists paid too much attention to security matters, and not enough to transnational connections, democracy, and international institutions and law.

In a way, both these critiques would be correct. To consider the field of security, neo-realism probably explains the existing situation better than liberalism does. But in other fields of life, neo-liberal theories are probably much better able to grasp what is going on. An important question concerns the precise relationships between these different fields. Does security matter more than global trade or international law? One attempt to answer this question came from a group of scholars positioned mainly outside the United States, which has dominated the study of international relations. This group is known as the international society school (or the English School of international relations), and its members tried to synthesize or join together realist analysis with liberal insights.

3-6 The international society school

A group of international relations scholars based mainly in Britain and Australia came up with an explanation of international relations that tried to synthesize or join together both realist insights and liberal insights into a more comprehensive framework. In the simplest possible terms, this approach suggested that the world was competitive and risky, just like the realists said, and also cooperative and progressive, just like the liberals said.

For example, the United Nations system was designed to achieve international peace and security through cooperation in especially collective security. But this organization clearly is by no means an ideal organization in which objective and rational thinking and decision-making from a global perspective are common. Rather, as symbolized by the fact that the United Nations Security Council's five permanent members were all on the winning side of World War II, and that they all try to use their special veto powers for their own state purposes, realist power politics by states is an integral part of the United Nations. But at the same time, the UN is also inclusive. Almost all states are members, and states have equal rights in, for example, the General Assembly. Rule-based procedures in which states participate as equals, solving conflicts through rational discussion and negotiation, are a part of the way that the United Nations operates, just as power politics is a part of the way that the United Nations operates.

A world at once realist and liberal

This particular example of the United Nations could be applied to the analysis of states. Virtually all states have militaries or self-defense forces, and they generally try to be as strong as possible, economically, politically, and militarily. If they see a chance of gaining benefits or increasing security by using their power over another state actor with few risks, it is likely that they will do so. However, states are also bound by law. They are unlikely to do anything in their search for security and economic benefits that is completely outrageous in terms of international law and domestic law. Power and state interests matter, in terms of what states do, but so do domestic opinion and international norms and institutions.

Even if the global system is anarchic, in this view, the states still make up a society that follows rules, despite the absence of a global government. This approach accepts that there is a need for some power, and some balancing of other states, because it is true that the system is anarchic, and leaders have a responsibility to guarantee the security of their people. Power is a key way to protect national security, as realists claim. However, against realism, the English school proposes that humans cooperate as much as they compete. We have shared rules and law not just at the domestic level, but at the international level too. Each state has a narrow responsibility to its people, but also bears a broad responsibility to the community of states that allows them to exist as a state. This responsibility includes such actions as following international law and participating in international institutions, as liberals recommend.

From the international society position, states are perhaps becoming secondary for certain types of actors and issues. For example, in the case of so-called failed states, where the central government is too weak to govern its own territory effectively, security is not a state matter, but rather a local issue. At the same time, for transnational communities with an interest in global issues such as trade, finance, environment, or disarmament, states may appear as obstacles to problem-solving, rather than the main actors.

From this brief overview of trends in the two major theories that tried to explain international relations through the twentieth century, it is possible to suggest that there are no universal laws that apply all the time to all situations and actors. Rather, the models we use to understand world affairs are always changing, because the world that we live in is always changing. Because the world is highly complex, no single model is able to comprehend all of reality. Different models are necessary to deal with different kinds of situations and actors, and it does not appear possible to say that any particular model is always and everywhere valid. One important lesson for us is this: the future world will not be like today's world, and so we will surely require new and different theoretical models to understand it.

N.M.

Questions

1.   In your own words, explain how changes in the world system are associated with changes in the theoretical frameworks used to think about the world system.

2.   Does the international society analysis successfully overcome the shortcomings of both neo-realism and neo-liberalism?

3.   Which theoretical position do you find most attractive? Why do you think this is? Explain with reference to your personal philosophy of life.

4.   Which theoretical position do you find least attractive? Why do you think this is? Explain with reference to your personal philosophy of life.

5.   Write a summary of the different theoretical positions sketched out in this chapter.

Chapter 4 Realist theories of international relations

"International politics, like all politics, is a struggle for power." Hans Morgenthau

Of the different theories that try to explain what happens in international relations, realism and neo-realism have been particularly influential. The key point in realist theories is the fact that the world system is made up of sovereign states, and so is anarchic. The fact that a system is anarchic does not mean that it is necessarily chaotic. It might be chaotic, or it could be orderly, but simply put, it means that there is no higher authority who is ultimately responsible for the maintenance of order in the system.

Basically, state sovereignty means that there cannot be authorities higher than the governments of states. Consequently, what states do cannot be controlled from above. As long as states do not violate the sovereignty of other states, this may not be an issue. But the problem is that there is no guarantee that states will respect the sovereignty of others.

In the real world, sovereignty is actually violated fairly frequently. To consider just the post-World War II era, the Soviet Union controlled the Baltic states of Latvia, Estonia and Lithuania, along with most of eastern and central Europe. More recently, its successor, Russia in 2014 took over parts of the Ukraine. The United States has an even more extensive record in the post-World War II era of violating the sovereignty of other countries, interfering in various countries in Latin America, Asia, Africa, Oceania, Europe, and the Middle East. Just in the last few years, its military has violated the sovereignty of Pakistan, Yemen, Somalia, Afghanistan, and Iraq.

Rules concerning state sovereignty are violated all the time, at least by strong actors like the United States and Russia. Given that there is no global police, the governments of powerful states obviously think they can get away with violating the sovereignty of weak states, such as the victimized states listed above, who don't have the capability to retaliate. Realist thinking focuses on how states should behave in these kinds of anarchic international conditions.

Most realists admit that interstate relations are generally orderly and law-abiding. However, the fact that violations of international rules do occur means that states should not be too optimistic about others acting according to the rules, whether in security matters in particular, or in policy matters more widely. They propose that states can't trust other states always to follow the rules, and so should prepare to deal with a range of undesired but possible risks involving aggressive action by other states.

Realist theories can be classed into two major types, classical realism which focuses on the idea that people and states are self-interested and power-seeking in an anarchic international system, and neo-realism, which claims that the problem is not so much due to human nature as to the nature of the anarchic world system itself. Common to both of these two major strands of realism is the idea that to assure the security of a state under anarchic conditions, it is important to maximize economic, political and especially military power.

4-1 Achieving security

Classical realists propose that human nature is the major factor making the world we live in dangerous. The basic concern is that like the political philosopher Thomas Hobbes claimed in his mid-17th century book Leviathan, human beings are essentially self-interested and power-seeking. Valuable resources such as money, power, security and prestige are scarce, and people compete to get them. In order to compete successfully, and to keep your winnings, it is necessary to obtain power.

If there is no authority that creates and maintains order, such as in early human societies, then violent and dangerous social conditions result, Hobbes argued. Anyone possessing valuable goods would be in danger of attack from others who also desire those goods. Strength would be the only way to assure security in such a society, where all other people are potential threats. In order to avoid living in this kind of dog-eat-dog society ruled by the law of the jungle, he argued that humans gave up some of their freedom or sovereignty by forming states in which the government would have the power to control or regulate

Chapter 4 Realist theories of international relations

people in a way that guaranteed security for all.

Admittedly, even within societies governed by states that provide at least a minimum of security and order, people will still try to promote their own interests and amass power. Richer and more powerful people may try to increase their wealth by getting poorer and weaker people to work for extremely low wages and or in bad working conditions (e.g., economic exploitation in "black companies"), just as historically, landowners forced people to work just for food and shelter without the freedom to change jobs (e.g., various forms of tenant farming and slavery).

In state-governed societies, there is therefore considerable variation in the level of security enjoyed by individuals. Some people are rich and powerful and well able to protect their own interests, while others are less influential and less able to live the life that they desire. But all the same, the existence of a state government makes life at least minimally secure. Faced with various forms of violence, it is possible to request and reasonably expect government assistance and protection.

However, state protection and assistance is limited. One can only reasonably expect a fairly minimal degree of protection. If classical realism's claim that humans are self-interested and power-seeking is true, or even if it is only partly true and just some humans are self-interested and power-seeking, inside states too, it is important for individuals to try and become as strong and as independent as possible, to prevent abuse and exploitation by others.

Achieving international security

Classical realism focuses not on individuals' lives within states, but on the relations between states in the international system. Classical realists propose that power and autonomy are even more important for states in the international system than for individuals within states, because while individuals at least have some protection offered by the state, states have no higher authority on which they can rely on in times of international conflict. In other words, although the law of the jungle is considered not to apply to life within states today, it is still seen to apply in interstate relations.

The classical realist position assumes that states are self-interested and power-seeking, like the human beings who form them. Although human societies have been able to create governments that maintain order and protect people's lives at the state level, such arrangements have not yet been created at the interstate level. And if even some states are like some humans in sometimes being selfish and power-seeking, then it makes sense for states to try to be as strong and as independent as possible, to prevent abuse and exploitation by other states.

To sum up, classical realism takes a pessimistic view of human nature, and of states, which are taken to resemble the people who create them. If all or some people are self-interested and power-seeking, then our security, even as individuals protected by states, requires that we engage in self-help as best we can. Individually, for example, a good education, a decent income, a supportive family, and a broad-ranging social network may be good ways in which a person could increase their own security, or their chances of living the sort of life that they aspire to, relatively free of domination or control by others.

If states are like humans in being self-interested and power-seeking, and yet are unregulated by any higher authority, then it is even more important that each state engage in self-help to assure its own own security. At the state level, having a wealthy economy, strong military, large and educated population, and a wide range of allies may be the main ways in which a state can increase its chances of security, and enjoy relative freedom from domination or control by others.

4-2 The Neo-realist theory of international relations

Neo-realist theories basically are the same as classical realist theories in stressing the importance of self-help and power for states so that they can assure their own security as far as possible. However, their reasoning is based on somewhat different assumptions. Neo-realists are less interested in claims about the nature of individual human beings. Instead, they are primarily concerned with the nature of the modern world system, and especially with the fact that the world system is anarchic.

As Hobbes pointed out, people enjoy a certain degree of security within states. We live with the expectation that violent crimes will be rare, that our individual safety, as well as the security of our homes and neighborhoods and cities, will be taken care of by the government. Of course, people in stable wealthy areas enjoy a much higher degree of security than those living in less stable areas suffering from unrest, where the general level of security is lower. But overall, it is clear that one of the key functions of states is to provide an orderly living environment for their populations. They do this through regulation and laws that are ultimately supported by legitimate force, or in other words, the police, legal system, military, and other institutions of government. Order at the domestic level is based on people accepting the rule of law enforced by the state because it is necessary for them to enjoy security in everyday life.

However, although states have legitimate authority over their inhabitants and can use their authority to maintain order internally, there is no legitimate authority that governs states internationally. Relations between states on the international stage are thus characterized by anarchy, or the absence of government. Remember that sovereign states are states in which the government is the highest legitimate authority. No organization or person stands above them, so legitimate force cannot be used to regulate aggression or other unacceptable behavior by states.

The risks of anarchy

Why would a state take aggressive action against other states, or otherwise violate international law? One reason is related to the fact that one of the main tasks of the state is to protect the interests of the people, and especially to assure their security.

National security is rarely defined clearly and precisely. Some leaders may feel that for their country to be truly secure, they need to have control not just over their own territory, but over neighboring territories too, in the way that the Soviet Union created an array of satellite states around it. Others may try to influence politics in surrounding states to prevent neighbors from forming alliances with unfriendly powers. An example of this may be found in the way that China gives limited support to the North Korean government in the hope that it doesn't collapse. Regime collapse would not only destabilize the East Asian region, but it might also lead to Korean re-unification. China would currently prefer to avoid this possibility, because it would likely mean having a close United States ally right on its borders, whereas North Korea today forms a kind of buffer zone between China and South Korea. To take another different kind of example, Israel feels that the development of nuclear weapons capability by Iran, whose government has repeatedly denied Israel's right to exist, would constitute a major threat, and so has in the past few decades used missile strikes and computer viruses to damage Iranian nuclear facilities and equipment.

In short, national security can be said to be directly connected to the situation of other states, and in particular to their level of military or economic power, the kinds of alliances that they have, and so on. Since these factors affect a state's ability to be autonomous and secure in international relations, some leaders will want to try and intervene outside of their borders, if possible, in order to protect what they see as their national interests.

For neo-realists, because we live in this anarchic system without a global government or organization holding the authority and the means of controlling the actions of other states, this kind of intervention is possible or even likely if a state considers that it has the ability to intervene elsewhere without running any major risks. In order to avoid being subjected to outside intervention, it is vital for states to be as strong and as self-reliant as possible, militarily, economically and politically. States need to try to maximize their economic and military and political power, to guarantee as best they can their continued independent existence.

4-3 The effects of realist thinking

Neo-realist thinking suggests that relationships between states in today's anarchic system are fundamentally driven by considerations of the national interest, and especially national security. States may develop close relationships with other states, if both sides feel that it is beneficial to cooperate. For example, they may form military alliances against a common threat, or engage in mutually profitable economic cooperation. However, such alliances and cooperation are limited, for a variety of reasons.

Changing relationships

Firstly, there is no guarantee that today's friend will be tomorrow's friend. Japan and Great Britain were allied states during the early part of the 20th century, but then fought against each other during the Second World War, for example. During the Cold War, the Mujahideen in Afghanistan received US support against the Soviet

Union, while today, as the Taliban, they are considered enemies of the United States. In an example of the opposite tendency, Japan and the United States fought against each other in World War II, but have now become close allies. Since friends and enemies will change according to evolutions in global conditions, it is better, realists would suggest, not to enter into too deep a relationship with other states, but to focus on gathering as much power individually as possible.

The problem of relative gains

Secondly, the aim of being as powerful as possible in order to assure security may discourage mutually beneficial cooperation, because of concerns about how the benefits of cooperation will be distributed. Cooperation will probably lead to overall benefits, or to absolute gains: all participants should be better off after cooperation than before. However, relative gains, or how the gains are distributed among participants, are of concern to realists. If the benefits are absolutely equally distributed, then there will have been little or no change in the power relationship between the cooperating participants. But if the benefits are unequally distributed, then the existing power balance will have shifted, to benefit some parties more than others. If another participant benefits more, economically or militarily, then the power relationship with that participant will have worsened. Thus cooperation in that case could be said to have had negative consequences on national security.

This concern with relative gains, or how benefits are distributed, together with the fact that allies and enemies are likely to change ceaselessly, means that realists are rarely completely enthusiastic about working with others. If state security is the most important goal, and state security involves maximizing economic and military power relative to other states, then any agreement that would allow other states to gain more power relative to your own state is problematic.

Trust in a world of self-interest

A further issue regarding cooperation is the problem of trust. If all states are self-interested and concerned with maximizing their own power, then any cooperative agreement would need to be considered in that light. That is, can states be trusted to keep their promises? Many realists, following the Italian writer Niccolo Machiavelli, argue that national security is the most important thing, and that ethics, morality, promises and so forth are secondary. From the standpoint of the national interest, it is permissible to break treaties and other kinds of promises, or to assassinate people or imprison people without due process. To cooperate with other states led by politicians who hold these kinds of ideas would call for great caution.

4-4 Criticisms of realist thinking

The claim by some realist thinkers that national security is all-important and justifies whatever acts that policy-makers find necessary to maintain it is controversial. Can decisions about right and wrong always be considered secondary to decisions about national security? Does survival have to be assured before consideration can be given to anything else? Many consider that it is hard to justify giving this kind of absolute value to state national security.

Are classical realists right about human nature?

An even broader critique of realism concerns the notion that humans and states are necessarily self-interested and power-seeking, either because of their nature, or because of the system that they exist within. In opposition to the idea that humans are fundamentally self-interested, there are innumerable examples of human beings sacrificing themselves for larger aims, ranging from religion—the most famous religious martyr is probably Jesus Christ—to nationalism, such as in the case of many of the military deaths in World War I and World War II. Other common cases include parents who die for their children, or children who sacrifice themselves for their family. People may even sacrifice themselves for unknown strangers, by trying to help people struggling in wild surf, by leaping down in front of onrushing trains to help people who have fallen off train platforms, or by intervening to assist strangers targeted by criminal violence.

The widespread nature of such cases, combined with the positive social evaluation given to such action, and the strong social sanctions against self-centered behavior, not to mention recent work on human psychology that proposes that we have an innate sense of justice or fairness, all indicate that the classical realist thesis about human nature is wrong.

Is power-maximization rational?

In the case of neo-realism, a fairly fundamental critique concerns the idea that states are rational actors who should seek to maximize power and autonomy to protect their own security in an anarchic system, and that in so doing they should minimize dependence on others, and limit cooperation because of the risk of relative gains for others. For one state to do this in the aim of maintaining and increasing its security against other states may appear rational. But if all states are engaged in trying to maximize their power against other states at the same time, then the overall result may be a vicious cycle of militarization and tension that leads to decreased security in the international environment. Realism in this sense may seem to be rational for individual states, but of limited rationality from a perspective that looks at the security of all members of the system.

Are policy-makers (and humans) rational?

Additionally, the neo-realist claim that states act in rational ways assumes, of course, that the individuals who conduct state policy-making are rational. But in reality, studies in human psychology show that while many societies do value reason more highly than emotion, this does not mean that our rational minds tightly govern our feelings. Rather, our emotions frequently win out over reason. The powerful emotions of nationalism and xenophobia, for example, often lead to irrational and ill-advised decision-making. Against neo-realist assumptions of human rationality, it is likely that we humans are emotional beings who often cannot control the way we feel. Because of this, the assumption that states are rational and unitary actors seems difficult to sustain.

Indeed, if a state's aim is to achieve security, then economic interdependence and international institutions seem to offer an alternative, more rational path towards that end, as supporters of international relations liberalism argue. Liberalism takes more seriously the possibility that international organizations and law and trade matter, and that domestic political arrangements make a difference to the behavior of states on the international stage. The construction of the European Union, for example, seems to offer a good example of actual behavior by states that cannot be explained in terms of the realist paradigm. Let us next consider the other major theoretical explanation of how states act in international relations, which is usually termed liberalism or liberal idealism.

N.M.

Questions

1.   Explain the key differences between classical realism and neo-realism.

2.   Do you agree with the realist position that state security should always be the first priority for policy-makers? Why or why not? Explain your answer using real-world examples.

3.   "Perfect security for one state is perfect insecurity for other states." What does this mean? What does it suggest about the nature of power-based security in an interstate system? Explain your response using examples.

4.   Using examples, explain your perspective on the criticisms of realist theories.

Chapter 5 Liberal theories of international relations

"Without man and his potential for moral progress, the whole of reality would be a mere wilderness, a thing in vain, and have no final purpose."
Immanuel Kant

Liberalism refers to a position in political philosophy that favors the maximum possible amount of individual freedom. It holds that people should be able to decide the kinds of lives that they desire to live by themselves, without any more pressure or intervention from the state than necessary. How much state intervention is necessary? One influential conception has been that proposed by Hobbes in his 1651 book Leviathan, in which he proposes that people's freedom should be limited by the state only to that extent necessary to protect people's security.

5-1 Progress through reason

Hobbes' argument was based on his assumption that people in ungoverned societies enjoyed absolute freedom, because they were not controlled by any higher authority. However, at the same time, those people were too insecure to enjoy that freedom, precisely because there was no higher authority. To resolve this problem, people created states with the authority to govern over people. This creation limited people's freedom somewhat, but it achieved security in return. Providing as much individual freedom as is compatible with general security can be said to be the core task of state governments.

That humans can achieve progress through the use of reason, as in this example of the creation of the state to safeguard both security and freedom, is a key idea in the liberal tradition. John Locke, a major figure in early liberal thought, wrote in the 17th century about the transition from feudal societies to modern societies as being a fundamentally progressive or desirable transition. As a result of the modernization of societies, human beings were moving from a system with little freedom or rights for most people, and the constant threat of private violence and exploitation, to a system in which states guaranteed equality and freedom to most people, with a capitalist economic system that allowed and indeed required various individual freedoms.

This belief in rational progress was also supported by the scientific revolution and modern technologies that allow people more control over nature, and increased productive powers. Given humanity's massive achievements and increasingly powerful capabilities, many liberals believe that people are capable of designing a political and economic system that will allow greater happiness, security and freedom for the greatest number of people. This objective may require modifying and re-inventing the state, or even the creation of new supra-state and sub-state institutions, according to the liberal viewpoint. Compared to realist thinking, this belief in constant progress represents a key difference.

The realist tradition recommends that states engage in self-help to ensure their own security, because they exist within an anarchic international system of self-interested sovereign states. It assumes that the existing sovereign state system is the ultimate or final form of human organization, and that it is too difficult to create new institutions, actors and structures that will increase the likelihood of peace. But the liberal tradition proposes that human society and its institutions are things that can and should be constantly improved, in order to promote human freedom and security.

International order

While noted more as a realist thinker than a liberal thinker, Hobbes himself noted that despite the creation of states that guaranteed security within states, anarchy or a lack of protection of states by a higher authority or government was still a problem at the international level. A major reason for this was that people under the protection of states felt relatively secure in their everyday life, and tended not to feel a strong need to create a global government. But in his view, some kind of international organization would be useful in regulating state behavior to achieve increased security among states. Just as people accepted limits to their freedom in return for increased security, Hobbes felt that it would be useful for sovereign states to accept limits to their freedom so that they could enjoy increased security.

This idea would later be advocated by other major philosophers such as Jean-Jacques Rousseau, who in the 18th century commented that making a congress of European states possessing military-backed authority to judge over interstate conflict would be perfectly rational.

Chapter 5 Liberal theories of international relations

Having a way to avoid war, with all its costs to life, infrastructure, and psychological wellbeing, would benefit all states. Such a system, Rousseau said, would need to be designed carefully, so that any "global government" did not become itself a kind of tyrannical regime dominating the entire world, and so ultimately decrease global freedom.

These concerns continue to be key parts of the liberal agenda in international relations today. The prominent liberal thinker John Rawls proposes that we need to create new institutions and rules to govern outlaw states, promote human rights, and assist troubled societies, while Thomas Pogge likewise suggests that we need democratic governments with stronger limits on sovereignty. In particular, to realize a peaceful and ecologically sound future, sovereign powers need to be dispersed upwards to supra-state organizations, and downwards towards particular communities within states, he argues.

Reform and improvement

Overall, liberal ideas about international relations are rather more optimistic in their approach to the human world than realist approaches, and assume that it is possible to take various positive actions that can make the international system less risky. Whereas realism states that we have to deal with the existing system conditions, liberalism proposes that we can improve those conditions. Liberal theories generally hold that it is possible to create environments that encourage people to act in socially desirable ways. Just as people can create states with effective power to enforce laws to guarantee domestic security, so too it should be possible for people to create state- and international-level institutions and arrangements that guarantee international security.

If these types of action are not just possible but also effective, then it is because human nature does not determine what people do. According to liberals, humans are not just power-seeking and self-interested beings, as classical realists seem to believe. Or to be more precise, people may be power-seeking and self-interested, but it is possible to create social, political, and cultural environments in which these tendencies are discouraged, and more desirable tendencies such as power-sharing and a stress on the common interest, are encouraged.

At the state level, this phenomenon can be seen every day. If many people feel that certain acts should be outlawed, then they may work together to bring about political and legal change to regulate those acts. A society in which there is a consensus that the abuse of aged persons is bad may develop education programs to promote awareness of aged persons' rights, as well as programs and laws to discourage violation of such rights. Through these kinds of actions, that society would create an environment in which the abuse of aged persons is discouraged and hopefully minimized. The same kind of principle can also work to encourage desired behavior. If a society feels that solidarity between its members is becoming weaker, or that family ties are not as strong as they should be, it may establish awareness campaigns in the media, or public education programs, to try and encourage stronger social and family ties.

Realists may say that such programs can only be effective because ultimately, they are based on the state's power to enforce such laws and standards. In their view, without the support of the state and its legitimate authority over people, liberal ideas would be ineffective. Thus for them, liberalism may work at the state or domestic level, but not at the international level. However, liberals say that similar types of action to create conditions that discourage undesirable actions and encourage desirable actions can work at the international level too, without being backed up by any legitimate authority that stands above the state.

It is possible to identify four main currents in liberal theories of international relations today. They are commonly known as sociological liberalism, interdependence liberalism, republican liberalism, and institutional liberalism.

5-2 Sociological liberalism: transnational communities

International relations, from the sociological point of view, is not just a matter of inter-state relations as it often is for especially realists. Individual people, sub-state groups and organizations, as well as transnational organizations and groups, are all actors on the world stage, engaged in cross-border social exchanges, cultural contacts, and scientific communication, or in other words, in mutually profitable relations that often provide examples of successful cooperation. This is significant because it is often considered easier for people to cooperate and engage in peaceful relations than it is for states to do so.

Transnational relationships

Among the significant thinkers in this particular liberal

Chapter 5 Liberal theories of international relations

tradition is Karl Deutsch, who in the 1950s engaged in the study of transnational relations. His work led him to suggest that communication and exchanges between societies created more connections, which increased the chances of peaceful relations across borders. This was because people who were connected to other people across borders by trade, communications and social ties came to develop a sense of togetherness. They became familiar with each other, benefitted mutually, shared a range of important values, and sometimes came to form a security community. That is, as they became closer together, they began to constitute a community in which members were likely to try to solve problems without using major force against other members. Rather, in conflicts between members, they would tend to discuss and negotiate and compromise to find peaceful solutions to common issues.

Communication, human mobility, economic exchanges and other transactions were positive factors that were helping to make this kind of community across the Atlantic, bridging North America and Western Europe, Deutsch proposed. Looking at the world since then, it seems likely that Deutsch would consider the constantly increasing number of connections between different parts of the world to be a highly promising trend, which should be encouraged.

Global networks

Another key figure in sociological liberalism is John Burton, who in his 1972 World Society used the analogy of societies as cobweb networks. In this model, many different groups and actors, including individuals, groups, associations, are connected to each other through various kinds of ties and interests, including religion, business, labor, and so on. In total, these different actors and the networks they participate in make up the state, which is therefore incredibly diverse and complex, and frequently connected in multiple ways across borders.

Compared to the realist model of a world made up of unitary state actors, this model tends to cast light not only on the fact that societies are internally diverse, but also on the point that communities rarely are limited by state political borders. Using Burton's approach to map the world according to the location of particular communities, or according to economic relationships or cultural interests, for example, would give us a view of a completely different world to that provided by a conventional state-centric political map.

Mapping the people connected by an interest in Japanese

popular culture, for example, animation or *manga*, would show us the outline of a truly global community spanning all states and continents, including people of various ages, ethnicities, and classes. In the same way, mapping the people connected by their participation in the production, circulation and consumption of Korean cars would reveal another, very different global network of interconnected actors. So too would the mapping of people connected by an interest in environmental sustainability, or the promotion of civilian nuclear power, and so on.

In short, the cobweb model indicates to us the existence of another world, which realists pay little attention to. In this world, real social, economic and cultural relationships and communities are not limited to the insides of state borders, but are all connected to each other in complex fashion, and unavoidably have effects, from below, on states and their international relations.

Complex interdependence

In these kinds of conditions of complex interdependence, say Keohane and Nye in their 1977 book Power and interdependence, the traditional approach that involves putting national security or high politics first, and economic and social affairs or low politics second, is no longer useful. Interstate relations have become more complex, involving intergovernmental organizations, non-governmental organizations such as consumer groups, producer groups, and multinational corporations. Not only are there more actors, but there are more levels too, as grassroots organizations interact with regional- and national-level organizations, as well as global-level organizations. The ideas and opinions of state leaders must take into account all of these various connections, as international politics becomes more and more like domestic politics in its complex diversity. Military force becomes less and less useful in interstate affairs, as alliances and agreements and coalitions cut across state borders, while non-military forms of power such as the ability to convince others through negotiation, diplomacy, soft power, and logic, become ever more important.

5-3 Interdependence liberalism: free trade and peace

Whereas sociological liberalism stresses the importance of cross-border social connections and communications, interdependence liberalism focuses primarily on the benefits of economic interdependence. It proposes that as the economies of the world become more and more integrated with each other, the risk of armed conflict tends to decrease. This argument comes from observation of how a division of labour makes people both wealthier and more interdependent, and how a modern division of labour, which may stretch all around the globe, makes people in different states wealthier and interdependent.

Economic modernization has involved industrialization, or manufacturing using fossil fuels and modern production technologies, to produce large amounts of standardized goods in a comparatively short time. A single factory specializing in the production of a limited range of products will be part of a long chain that connects the producers of raw materials, machines, parts, and fuel, as well as the transporters of such goods, the factory workforce, the distributors, consumers, and of course the various parties involved in the recycling and disposal industries.

A global division of labor

Today, it is common for some or even all of these different links in the chain to be positioned in different countries. Chinese factories may use Australian coal, Japanese machinery and locally sourced chemicals to produce plastic goods that are exported for sale in the European Union. After use, these goods may be transported to countries in Africa for waste reprocessing. In this kind of example, the production, distribution, consumption, and disposal of goods makes countries dependent on each other, to obtain currency, jobs, profits, goods and services. This kind of global division of labour is, in short, a case of cooperation for mutual benefit. It helps overall levels of prosperity to rise, due to specialization and associated gains in efficiency and productivity.

Today, this kind of interdependence is not limited to primary industries and factory-produced goods, but also extends to the case of services. For example, American insurance companies operating in Japan may use call centers in north-eastern China, just as Japanese companies doing business in the United States may rely on call centers in the Philippines, as well as on information technology experts in India.

If states are connected to each other through trade networks that cut across national boundaries, they become economically interdependent. They come to depend on each other to get necessary goods and services. At the same time, people on both sides become materially more wealthy.

Economics against war

War, which disrupts trade routes and upsets global financial markets, would have a generally negative effect on trade, and so on states' economic situations. It also would be undesirable for consumers within those states, as well as for the politicians who depend on the electoral support of those consumers who vote. It would also be undesirable for the corporate elites and their employees whose profits and salaries respectively depend on the continuity of global trade processes. As states become involved in a global division of labor, and as their populations become wealthier and thus have more to lose from involvement in wars, they become more likely to try and avoid the various risks of armed conflict and war.

Neo-liberal theories about interdependence basically suggest that the higher the level of interdependence, the lower the risk of armed conflict should be, because rational actors who benefit from the existing system would want to keep those benefits. At the same time, it is possible to reason that logically, the less integrated areas of the world have a higher risk of armed conflict. And this is basically what we see today: there seems to be little possibility of conflict between the most highly integrated areas of Western Europe, North America, and East Asia. On the other hand, there is considerable violence in less developed countries where the level of economic interdependence with other areas of the world is very low.

The promotion of free trade

Given that trade seems to be not just economically beneficial, but also a factor that discourages war, the more trade there is, the better, says liberal theory. In order to maximize trade connections around the world and economic interdependence, trade ought to be as free as possible. States should lower customs duties and import tariffs, and dismantle non-tariff barriers to trade by adopting unified standards on consumer protections, environmental conservation, carbon emissions, chemicals in food production and so on. Such measures, if they become universal, should lead to the maximum possible amount of trade around the world. In such a globalized world, conflict in one place would never just be a matter for the direct participants. If all countries are connected to each other in a global trading network, conflict anywhere becomes something that is generally undesirable for the global community. Such a development should help to make the world a safer place.

5-4 Republican liberalism: democracy and peace

According to republican liberalism, another way to improve the chances of international peace is the promotion of democracy, taken to be a form of political government in which the majority of people, based on good information and free from pressure or coercion, are able to vote for their own preferred political representatives from a range of candidates who compete against each other based on ideas and policies on a level playing field.

In complex modern societies, this kind of system usually leads to a range of diverse groups being represented in government, since people tend to be relatively diverse in terms of values and concerns. Further, because majority support is necessary to make laws and regulations, important decisions tend to require discussion and compromise between a range of different political actors.

Popular sovereignty against war

So long as no particular groups dominate a society, and power is relatively evenly distributed, then this kind of system is considered to lower the risk of that society commencing an aggressive war. This is because most wars involve massive sacrifices of people and property, not to mention that they have immense negative effects on people's sense of wellbeing and security. Wars tend to be risky affairs, and voters tend to be risk-averse. Because of this, wars are generally unpopular with many people, and with a range of political parties, especially if there appears to be little chance of a quick and successful end to conflict. Given that political leaders in democracies depend on gaining the support of at least some opposition parties, and of voters at elections held every few years, the likelihood of democratic states going to war is therefore seen to be small.

Conversely, republican liberalism proposes that when political power is highly concentrated within a democratic state, being dominated by a small group, the risk of aggressive action rises, especially if war is seen to be in the interests of that small dominant group. This principle applies even more to the case of authoritarian states. Given that their governments do not have to be greatly concerned with elections and popular support, and that power is dominated by a relatively small group, the risk that they will engage in aggressive action is seen to be relatively higher than in the case of democratic states.

Peace as a core value

From the viewpoint of republican liberalism, in states with democratic political systems, not just politicians but also the general public are accustomed to conflict taking place only in words, with physical violence being considered fundamentally illegitimate, or as morally inferior and shameful behavior. Decision-making is another term for negotiation and compromise.

Democratic process

States that have a domestic culture of democratic politics are considered likely to follow these kinds of procedures in international politics too. This is partly because voters in democratic states are unlikely to accept undemocratic procedures and violence as legitimate in international politics, if they find those things unacceptable in domestic politics. This is especially likely in the case of two or more democratic states, who share the tendency to put a high value on peaceful negotiation, and to deny the validity of violence as a tool of foreign policy. Thus the promotion of democratic governments around the world should lead to an increase in the number of states who follow democratic principles in their international relations. This, liberals say, is one of the most important ways in which the international environment might be made safer.

5-5 Institutional liberalism: international organizations and law

James Rosenau, a major liberal theorist, argues that the rise of new global issues that affect all people, such as environmental pollution and degradation, rapid and unstable financial flows, international crime, mass migration, civil wars, failed states and so on mean that we need, more than ever, effective international institutions of governance. In effect, liberal theory has long placed much more importance than realist theory on international organizations and rules.

As networks involving transnational communication and interdependence deepen and widen, more and more international institutions have been emerging to help deal with common problems

Chapter 5 Liberal theories of international relations

ranging from disease and food supply to monetary stability and defense. By making it easier for states to discuss issues and conflicts and share information, by reducing uncertainty about what other states intend or are doing, and by providing rules and guidelines for conflict resolution, such institutions are considered to enable and encourage states to cooperate, and so to enhance international peace and security. The theoretical approach that stresses the importance of these kinds of international institutions in achieving a more peaceful world system is known as institutional liberalism.

International institutions

The term "international institution" can refer to international governmental organizations such as NATO, the European Union, ASEAN, and so on, which are formed by governments to deal with common military, political, economic, financial, social and cultural issues. It can also refer to something more abstract. Sets of rules governing state action in a particular area, such as telecommunications or fisheries or nuclear technology, may be referred to as an institution or a regime. These rules may be written down, as in the Nuclear Non-Proliferation Treaty that governs the possession and use of civilian and military nuclear materials and technology, or they may be customary rules that are influential just because they have been followed for a long time, such as the set of ideas associated with the balance of power. Sometimes they are associated with particular organizations—the NPT is associated with the IAEA, for example—while sometimes they are not, as in the case of balance of power.

The case of Europe

An important case often used to discuss the viewpoint of institutional liberalism is European integration. EU member countries share common agricultural and industrial policies, basic legal standards for human rights and environment, money, and so on. European-level institutions make sure that information is shared between member states, and also that they can negotiate with each other as needed. They also allow governments to check each other's actions, and make sure that they all are doing what they have agreed to do. This function makes it possible in the first place to make promises and agreements: knowing that you can check that others will keep to the agreements, and that others will be able to check that you are keeping to the agreements too. As these institutions work effectively, they reinforce people's

confidence that they are useful and necessary.
Institutional influences

Another important thing about international institutions is the influence that they can have, in some conditions, over member states, and prospective member states. For example, institutions such as the World Bank and the IMF can encourage states to democratize, reduce military control over politics, and engage in more free trade as conditions for receiving loans and development assistance. Collective defense organizations such as NATO can encourage states that wish to join to similarly become more democratic and accountable. International institutions in this way can help countries to become more democratic, or more economically integrated with other countries, and so less likely to engage in aggression in their international relations.

Overall, the more such institutions prove effecting in assisting cooperation, democratization and free trade, the more they reinforce the idea that world politics is not a zero-sum game with clear winners and losers, but rather can be a win-win game in which the aim of participants is not to defeat or dominate others, but to work together with them to create a better world. Successful coordinated action such as by the United Nations in peace-building or the maintenance of order, for example, helps also to build trust and optimism in a brighter future, and of course, higher levels of international trust and optimism can lead to more cooperation, in a virtuous circle.

5-6 Evaluating liberal theories of international relations

From the viewpoint of many realists, liberal theorists are misguided in their focus. Even if states contain many different groups with varying interests, the primary interest remains the achievement of national security against other states. Whatever political party comes to power, it remains true that their policy-making decisions will prioritize security. Thus sociological liberalism and interdependence liberalism give too much importance to phenomena of secondary importance.

Republican liberalism has been criticized from a different perspective. Although it is true that liberal democratic states have never gone to war with each other, liberal democratic states have gone to war against non-democratic states. In at least some cases, the decision to go to war appears to have been made by political leaders who calculated

Chapter 5 Liberal theories of international relations

that a short war could raise their popularity among voters, who tend to vote for the governing party in times of war, and so boost their chances of re-election.

An important realist critique of postwar liberal theories of international relations concerns the argument international institutions have made the world safer. Considering how the United Nations was greatly restricted in terms of the action it could take during the Cold War, or during the 2014 Crimea crisis, or the very limited progress of the Nuclear Non-Proliferation Treaty, it can be argued that international institutions are of relatively minor importance. Not only that, but institutions such as the World Bank and even the United Nations are clearly arenas of state power politics, even as they are supposed to be the center of cooperation and coordination in the global interest.

However, even if they are not backed up by higher authorities, and membership is freely chosen and can be freely given up, institutions and law backed by peer sanctions can be effective on the international stage. This is because trade, development cooperation, loans and investment, joint defense arrangements and other kinds of ties may depend on a state's reputation. States that are law-abiding and reliable will find it much easier to develop mutually profitable relationships with others than states that have reputations for being unreliable and frequently violating international law.

Overall, it seems clear that the world is increasingly interdependent, socially connected, and democratic, and that these factors can be significant in reducing the risk of interstate armed conflict. Further, international institutions that assist cooperation between states also appear to help reduce the risk of aggressive or illegal state actions. The continuing development of a body of international law and international institutions to govern economics, society, culture, finance and security can help to make the world a safer place. From the perspective that human reason can achieve global progress for humanity in terms of increased safety and freedom, therefore, liberals propose the continued promotion of free trade and communication, democratization, and international institutions.

N.M.

Questions

1. How much do you agree with the liberal belief in the possibility of progress, cooperation, and peace? Why?

2. Explain why (a) limiting individual freedom by creating states and thereby achieving domestic security, is more difficult than (b) limiting state sovereignty by creating global institutions to achieve systemic security.

3. Are the four strands of liberalism all equal in importance? What is the significance of the recent economic development of non-democratic trading states such as Singapore and China?

4. Compare and contrast the realist and liberalist theories of international relations.

5. Explain how international institutions may help keep the peace in international relations. Give examples.

Whole class / group activity

• Investigate the number of ongoing conflicts in the world today: make a list of the state actors involved, and check to see their position on the list of democratic states at www.freedomhouse.org .

• Is there a tendency for violence to take place in less democratic states?

• What kinds of armed conflict are the more democratic states involved in?

Chapter 6 Marxist and neo-Marxist theories of international relations

"The history of all hitherto existing society is the history of class struggles."
Karl Marx

Realism examines international relations from the point of view of sovereign states in an anarchic system, and proposes that states need to engage in self-help to ensure their security. As for liberalism, it considers that anarchic relations between sovereign states can be made less risky by building institutions and norms that discourage war and encourage democratic and peaceful conflict resolution. By contrast, radical theories are strongly influenced by the work of Karl Marx, and look at the world from a very different angle: that of inequality, and economic inequality in particular. This inequality is seen to be one of the key factors affecting what happens in the international system.

6-1 Modes of production

Karl Marx was a European philosopher of economic, social and political history. Although Marx's work can hardly be summarized in a few paragraphs, for our purposes, it is significant that he considered that different types of economy—what he called modes of production— gave rise to different forms of social and political organization.

Marx noted that hunter-gather groups, because survival depended on helping each other out in materially poor and variable environmental conditions, tended to be cooperative and relatively democratic. By contrast, agricultural systems had higher levels of wealth, which tended to allow greater material inequality, and led to the development of landed aristocracy and royalty. Agricultural societies were thus often more hierarchical and top-down, with ordinary people enjoying less political influence.

Marx considered that the modern era's capitalist industrial societies, which depend on manufacturing goods for profit by selling them in a relatively free market, were characterized primarily by a division between those termed capitalists, who have relatively more ownership over capital—land, factories, technology and so on—and those termed workers, who do not and must sell their labor to make a living.

This economic gap shaped modern democratic political systems. These tended to have, for example, separate and opposed political parties, one representing the interests of the capitalist class, and another that represented the interests of the working class. This economic gap also shaped modern societies, which have working classes characterized by working class culture, and middle and upper classes characterized by middle-class and upper class culture.

Class conflict

Marx saw a fundamental problem in the power gap between capitalists, who had enough money or land or specialized skills to make a relatively independent living, and workers, who did not have enough of anything, and so had to make a living by selling their labor to other, wealthier people. The problem as Marx saw it was that the interests of the two groups were fundamentally opposed, while their power differed greatly. An example commonly used to describe this point comes from the period around the beginning of the industrial era in Britain and Europe more generally.

At this time, the rationalization of agricultural production—through mechanization, an increased emphasis on profit, and the introduction of more intensive cropping—saw farm management increase production while reducing the number of workers on the land. Many people who lost their jobs on farming estates had to look elsewhere for paid work, so that they could keep on living. Often they moved to the newly industrializing cities, where they tried to make money by selling their labor to factory owners.

Marx characterized the relationship between factory-owning capitalists and labor-selling proletarian workers as being one of exploitation. The aim of the capitalists was to maximize their profits by keeping production costs—for example, salaries and other worker benefits—as low as possible, while setting prices as high as the market would bear. The aim of workers, it hardly needs pointing out, was to get as decent a salary as possible, so that they could provide themselves and their families with a reasonable material life, and try to provide their children with educational and social resources that would allow

Chapter 6 Marxist and neo-Marxist theories of international relations

them to move on up the economic ladder when they became adults.

The reproduction of inequality

Although Marx identified a whole range of problems relating to equality, decency, and human dignity within the conflict between capitalist and worker, one pressing issue was the obvious power disparity between the two sides. Certainly, capitalists relied on workers to generate profits. But generally, the supply of workers exceeded the capitalists' need for workers. This meant that capitalists held the upper hand over workers in wage negotiations.

Workers' wages tended over time to remain around about at the level necessary to obtain housing and support a family. But they rarely reached a level at which the children of workers could expect to move out of the working classes.

On the other hand, the income levels of capitalists were such that their children could expect not only to remain at their station, but indeed, to become richer. A key problem that Marx analyzed was the fact that socio-economic position was unlikely to vary greatly through generations, with the capitalist classes able to arrange the socio-economic and political system to their own advantage through the use of their wealth to influence not just politics but also culture and society. While Marx has been especially influential in thinking about economics and society, a range of theorists have used his insights to think about the nature of the modern international system.

6-2 Lenin on capitalism and imperialism

The early-twentieth century Russian intellectual and political leader Vladimir Lenin theorized that the nature of industrial capitalism led directly to imperialism and colonialism, which were strategies for the leading capitalist states to dominate weaker states in a way that helped to increase their political and economic power. While it might be true that imperialism might also be somewhat driven by states' desire for the prestige that came from having a colonial empire, and that such empires might also help states in achieving security, Lenin proposed that the primary cause was economic.

Issues in industrial capitalism

Industrial capitalism allowed capitalists within the most advanced countries to produce goods in greater quantities and at higher

81

speeds than ever before. The potential to manufacture large quantities of goods in a short space of time came, however, with special constraints.

Firstly, to increase outputs required increased inputs as well. Raw materials were sometimes available domestically—coal and wool were plentiful in Great Britain, for example—but often it was more cost-effective to source materials from other places where living standards and salaries were lower, or resources were more plentiful.

Secondly, increased production with expensive machinery in high-technology factories faced the problem of finding sufficiently large markets for those goods. As the population in industrial societies became wealthier and consumed more goods, they could absorb some of the increase in production. But in the case of more durable goods such as steel goods, furniture, tableware and so on, domestic markets quickly became saturated.

Production capacity overtook consumption capacity, such that manufactured products could not be limitlessly consumed by customers within the advanced states alone. This became a large problem, as industrial production processes spread throughout the European region, and often led to different countries producing similar goods. In order to recoup the costs of setting up factories, and make enough money to re-invest in infrastructure and product development, which were necessary to keep on making a profit, it was vital for capitalists to find new external markets to sell their products.

Thirdly, as consumers in the European and North American industrial societies became wealthier and more sophisticated, they developed a taste for items that could only be acquired in far-off and often tropical zones of the world, such as tea and coffee, cacao beans and sugar, pepper and coffee. This led to a higher degree of interest in trading relations with these areas.

To sum up, the desire of industrial capitalists for more and cheaper resources, bigger markets, and new and desirable products, acted as the driving force of Western imperialism, argued Lenin. In other words, economic forces drove the integration of the world economy, through imperialism.

Imperialism as the answer

European imperialism, based on the economic wealth of

Chapter 6 Marxist and neo-Marxist theories of international relations

industrial capitalism twinned with the political and military power of centralized sovereign states with national militaries, provided a single solution to the various economic issues associated with industrial capitalism. Advanced industrial states took over "backward" regions of the world in Africa, the Middle East, Asia and Oceania. Denying these regions sovereignty on the grounds that their political formations were less advanced than those of Europe, they used them as resource stores, exclusive markets for manufactured goods, and production centers for desirable agricultural products to be marketed and consumed in the advanced regions of the world.

In this kind of colonial economic relationship, it is considered that the empires generated much greater economic benefits for themselves than they did for the colonies. Further, indigenous political structures in colonies were often damaged by the fact of outside control, while their societies were negatively affected by the introduction of racist ideologies and beliefs. Even if colonial development sometimes involved investment in transport, energy, and communications infrastructure, such investments were aimed at increasing the empire's ability to economically exploit their colonial territories. These points suggest some of the main reasons why former colonies stayed poor in the post-independence ere: their political systems, social systems, and economic systems had been overturned and re-tooled to meet the needs of Western imperial rulers. Unsurprisingly, the impact of these massive changes was not something that could be overcome immediately, and just with the assistance of political independence.

6-3 Dependency theory and world-systems theory

One reason that empires had originally acquired colonies was to solve the problem of industrial overproduction. Because of this, it is hardly surprising that colonial powers did not encourage the industrialization of their colonies. However, even after independence, few former colonies industrialized and improved their economic situations. To a large degree, this was because of the continuing influence of colonial-era trade patterns.

Just as many colonies had produced relatively cheap primary goods using low-cost labor and provided them to the rich imperial countries, so too did independent former colonies sell relatively cheap primary goods using low-cost labor to the rich former imperial countries. An important reason why their products were cheap is that overall, there tend to be more producers of goods such as bananas, spices, fish, coconut oil and so on than there are buyers, and so buyers have greater leverage than sellers in the global market. On the other hand, there are fewer producers of desirable finished goods, and more buyers, so that in this case sellers have relatively greater leverage than buyers in the global market.

Dependency theory

One problem caused by this situation was that the newly independent countries that exported relatively inexpensive goods tended to be consumers of relatively expensive goods, including machinery, weapons, and other manufactured goods produced in industrialized countries. This unequal exchange, of cheap goods for expensive goods, attracted attention from neo-Marxist scholars such as Raul Prebisch in the 1950s, and Immanuel Wallerstein and Andre Gunder-Frank in the 1970s and 1980s. They argued in the 1960s and 1970s that many former colonies remained poor even after independence because of their dependence on industrialized countries for manufactured goods which they couldn't produce by themselves. Their work developed Lenin's early-twentieth century idea that a world economy divided into core zones and peripheral zones had emerged, and that in this system, the core zones tended to exploit the peripheral zones.

World systems theory

Perhaps the most influential of these scholars was Wallerstein, who developed a theoretical framework commonly known as world-systems theory that categorized the contemporary world into core regions and peripheral regions, as well as semi-peripheral regions. Generally speaking, the core regions were democratic, with high levels of wages, investment, and welfare. These regions tended to import raw materials, and export manufactured goods. By comparison, the peripheral regions tended to be non-democratic, and to have low levels of wages, no welfare, and low levels of investment. They tended to export raw materials, and import manufactured goods. In between the two, he positioned semi-peripheral regions, which were characterized as having some characteristics of core regions, and some characteristics of peripheral regions. Such regions often had authoritarian governments, and low levels of wages and welfare. The semi-periphery engaged in

Chapter 6 Marxist and neo-Marxist theories of international relations

both the import and export of raw materials, as well as the import of manufactured goods. However, having its own industrial base, the semi-periphery also exported mature manufactures, or products made using standard technology.

Wallerstein's world-system theory offered a way to understand not just the unequal exchanges between industrialized and non-industrialized regions of the world, but also to grasp the fact that some states could become industrialized. The semi-periphery provided a new home for industries that had become uneconomic in the core states, such as car assembly or textiles. They also provided a source of migrant labor for core states, and provided some legitimacy for the existing economic system by providing a possible pathway to development for peripheral countries.

However, it is important to remember, as Wallerstein points out, that in a capitalist system that involves a fundamental opposition between workers and capitalists, as well as between core regions and peripheral regions, it is not possible for all states to achieve economic equality, just as it is not possible for all people to enjoy economic parity. As he says, relative positions of individual states in the structure of the world system may change, but the hierarchical structure itself stays in place. In short, radical theories of world politics suggest that international relations will be forever conflictual, so long as they take place within a capitalist world economy based on economic inequalities.

N.M.

Questions

1. Some propose that a core contradiction of capitalism is that low wages for workers can mean higher profits for capitalists, while capitalists also need well-paid workers to consume the products that are offered for sale in the market. Does the fact that the capitalist system is international provide a kind of answer to this contradiction?

2. What evidence can you offer in support of the idea that the core benefits at the expense of the periphery? What evidence can you offer against the idea that the core benefits at the expense of the periphery?

4. Do workers in rich countries and workers in poor countries have opposing interests? Is it possible for them to share a common interest?

5. Are dependency theory and world-systems theory useful to understand the contemporary world-system? Explain your answer using examples.

Small group / whole class activity

Choose four of the world's poorest countries, and four of the world's richest countries, and four of the world's newly industrializing countries, and examine their economic activity in terms of exports by value and category, and imports by value and category. Do the results tend to support dependency theory / world-systems theory, or do they also point to other possibilities?

https://www.cia.gov/library/publications/the-world-factbook/

http://data.worldbank.org/data-catalog/world-development-indicators

http://stat.wto.org/CountryProfile/WSDBCountryPFHome.aspx?Language=E

Chapter 7 Constructivism in international relations theory

"Anarchy is what states make of it." Alexander Wendt

Constructivist theories propose that what actors do in the world depends on how they see and understand themselves and others and the situation that they are in. Human perceptions and understandings, of self, other, context, and the actions that are appropriate, are not something absolute and ahistorical. Rather, they are created and evolve through human interaction, with people influenced by and influencing others in a dynamic process.

Constructivism has developed out of academic disciplines such as philosophy and sociology. One important figure is the philosopher Immanuel Kant, who wrote about how all knowledge is necessarily subjective, because it relies on human perception and consciousness. It is not how the world is objectively, but how people perceive the world, that matters, given that people take action based on particular meanings and understandings. Another is Max Weber, one of the founders of the discipline of sociology. He argued that the human world is fundamentally different from the natural world because people act in society based on the understandings that they have of themselves and others, and because these understandings are constantly changing through interaction between human beings.

Building on these intellectual traditions, Anthony Giddens has set out what he called a theory of structuration. Giddens proposes that social structure, by which he meant social positions, roles, and associated norms and values, do not determine people's actions in the social world in any mechanical way. Rather, people learn meanings and develop understandings in dynamic relations with other people. This makes meaning and understanding basically fluid and flexible, since people grow up and live in a wide range of different situations or contexts that produce meanings and understandings that vary widely.

It is obviously true that to some extent, meanings and understandings must be shared throughout societies to make social life predictable, orderly, and possible. But differences constantly arise, as some people always push against established truths and received wisdom, challenge existing authorities, and reject established norms and values. When such differences become particularly widespread, or when many people come to think about and understand society in new ways, then social structure and society itself may change.

The significance of this perspective in international relations is obvious. It suggests that we need to consider realism and liberalism, for example, not as simple objective descriptions of the world as it is and how states should act within it, but as socially constructed interpretations of the world. Those theories don't tell us how the world really is. They tell us how certain realists or certain liberals understand the world, and the reasons why they recommend that actors should behave in a particular way in the world. But their understandings and policy recommendations are socially constructed—they come out of a particular context and particular human interaction—they are not valid for all of history and all situations. Rather, they are relative and variable.

Alexander Wendt, a well-known constructivist scholar of international relations, wrote about anarchy that it is not a single objective situation with a clear meaning. In fact, it is a concept that can and sometimes does mean different things to different people. Whether a majority comes to understand anarchy as a dangerous war-prone condition or as a situation in which cooperation and mutual benefits are achievable depends on the social interaction between actors in different societies. Further, depending on the understanding of anarchy that becomes dominant in a particular time and place, and the actions that flow on from it, the international system may be tense and conflicted, or relatively settled and peaceful.

7-1 Social constructionism

To begin, it may be useful to set out a brief outline of the way that constructivists understand the relationship between society and individuals. Human beings are born as a kind of blank slate. Unable to move very much, or to communicate very much, or to protect ourselves, even, we are capable of very little, to begin with. Only as we learn language, values, rules, and so on through socialization by the society that we are born into, and only as we very slowly mature, do we start to become individual human beings with a sense of self.

We develop a sense of self through interaction with our parents, sisters and brothers, friends, classmates, teachers and so on. At the same time, in these interactions, we gain a sense of what it is to be ourselves—what is expected of us, what actions will bring disapproval, what actions will make others happy, what we are not allowed to do. We also gain an idea of what it is to be others—what friends or teachers are, what is expected of them, what they are allowed to do, and how they may stop being friends or teachers if they break particular rules.

We also learn something about how context makes a difference to who we are and what we and others do. Who we are at home is quite different from who we are at school, or at our part-time jobs. What we are expected to do in these different locations, and what we expect of others in each context, will be different.

Consider this example: Your family runs a business from home, and you are paid to work for two afternoons a week. Behavior that might be accepted during non-working times in the family home—sleeping, surfing the internet, talking to friends on the phone—becomes unacceptable during the hours that you are paid to work. For that time only, your home becomes your workplace, and members of your family become your colleagues. For different social positions with different social roles, you learn to follow different set of rules regarding behavior.

Freedom and social change

Importantly, this perspective on actions in society says that each individual has a certain amount of freedom when it comes to deciding how they meet the expectations placed on them. You can consider that every child's parents basically have the same job: to raise their child into an independent adult who is integrated in society. But within that framework, some parents are strict, others are relaxed; some treat their children like friends, others are more distant, and so on. Being aware of a range of possibilities, each parent has some degree of freedom of choice regarding their particular parenting style. If some parents come to understand vertical and emotionally distant relationships with their children as being undesirable, they may take action to develop more intimate and horizontal relationships inside the family. If this becomes a trend, then social structure, or the social positions of "parent" and "child", will both change somewhat. What it means to be a parent, and what it means to be a child, will shift, and the kinds of behavior that are expected or required will be different. Society

89

itself will change as a result.

Seen from this kind of perspective, society shapes who we are and what we do. However, it does so through the medium of social interaction—that is, people transmit common ideas and understandings to each other, in variable forms. This fact that we ourselves are agents of society at the same time that we are objects of society, means that we shape the wider society itself at the same time that it shapes us. This framework can also be used to think about the international order.

7-2 Constructivism in international relations: transformations in the Sinocentric East Asian order

When applied to international relations, constructivism proposes that something similar goes on. How states act comes down to how people—policymakers, bureaucrats, media, the public—understand concepts such as power, state, security, anarchy, nation, and so on, as well as how they see their own state, and other states. These understandings of identities and meanings (expectations, obligations and so on) are developed through interaction in society with other people. Identities and the expectations and obligations associated with them change through time, as the contexts in which states exist evolve. An example from Japan's early-modern and modern history will help to illustrate these points.

The Sinocentric order

The East Asian region of today was once covered by a Sinocentric system dominated by China. This system was made up of a core civilized state—the Middle Kingdom—surrounded by an array of semi-civilized vassal states such as Japan, Vietnam and Korea. On the periphery were positioned people from South-East Asian islands, indigenous mountain peoples of Taiwan, and so on, who were classed as barbarian because of their unfamiliarity with civilization as defined by Chinese standards.

Vassal states were largely autonomous, provided they paid tribute to the empire. In return, they received various trading rights and reciprocal gifts, as well as recognition of their government as legitimate by the Chinese emperor. Interstate relations within this system were largely limited to ceremonial visits by diplomatic representatives, and trade relations. As for the situation of ordinary people, in the states of

Chapter 7 Constructivism in international relations theory

the time, they were simply subjects of the emperor or the various kings of each state, excluded from political activity. Matters of government were decided exclusively by the ruling strata.

From a constructivist viewpoint, what we should note from the above is that the interactions between members of the ruling and intellectual strata of Japan, Korea and China, for example, determined how the rulers of each state understood their position, as well as their rights and obligations towards their own subjects, and towards other states with whom they had diplomatic relations. These understandings about interstate relations in the Sinocentric sphere, it hardly needs to be said, were not static. They changed considerably through time, due to the actions of other actors, and changes in the world-historical circumstances of these actors as well. This can be confirmed easily by looking at transformations in the way that Japanese intellectuals and leaders saw themselves, as well as China and Korea.

Position in the Sinocentric regional hierarchy was supposed to be dependent on how closely a state or people met the Confucian requirements for being a civilized and moral society, as revealed notably by the presence of stable and benevolent government. During Japan's early-modern period, perceiving a high level of domestic unrest in China, and noting the stability achieved under the Tokugawa military government, Japanese intellectuals associated with the ruling strata began claiming that Japan had become more civilized than China, and thus should be recognized as holding the highest position in the regional order. Similar trends developed in Korea too, where the authority of the Chinese emperor was increasingly placed into question. As a result, Japanese and Korean attitudes and actions towards China changed. In Japan, a strong anti-Chinese prejudice appeared, along with a sense of superiority towards Korea. These understandings would allow and encourage late nineteenth century Japanese aggression against Korea and China, leading up to the Sino-Japanese and Russo-Japanese wars of 1894-1895 and 1904-1905.

From a constructivist viewpoint, shifts in the way that Japanese rulers viewed themselves and Korea and China involved changes in their perception of mutual obligations and expectations. These changes allowed Japan's rulers to move from a stance of deep respect and even subservience towards China, to a stance of superiority and dominance.

From the Sinocentric order to a Westphalian order

This intellectual shift, whose real-world effects culminated in Japanese formal colonial control over the Korean peninsula, and effective control over large parts of China, was also partly the result of another intellectual transformation affecting Japan through the second half of the nineteenth century. Before the mid-nineteenth century, the actors in the Sinocentric system had no sense of being sovereign states. The European concept of sovereignty was unfamiliar to them. However, from the mid-nineteenth century onwards, the coming of European and North American sovereign states into the Asian region helped not just to bring about changes in the hierarchy of the Sinocentric system, but to destroy it completely.

Seeing China brought under the political control of especially Britain during the first half of the nineteenth century, Japan was the first Asian country to perceive and successfully respond to the threat of Western imperialism. The threat was posed superficially by the advanced military and organizational technologies possessed by the West. But at a deeper level, the contest between the Western powers and the Eastern powers was unequal because the West's capabilities were enhanced by the fact that their military, economic, financial and social resources were united under centralized governments. Further, non-Western states were placed at a disadvantage because these Western sovereign states only applied the principle of sovereignty to other "advanced" states like themselves. Political organizations in other areas of the world, such as Africa, Asia and Oceania, were denied the status of sovereign states, making it possible for them to be colonized and dominated without violating the principle of state sovereignty.

Japan's transformation into a sovereign state

The Japanese response, confronted by this new set of ideas about what a state was, and what kinds of rights, obligations and powers it could have, was to to try to achieve recognition as a sovereign state equal to the Western powers. This required increasing its power potential by revolutionizing the domestic political situation, and in particular, creating a centralized government, single economy and military, and a unified people or nation.

Concretely, this involved eliminating the decentralized feudal Tokugawa system, in which the lords of the 300 or so different domains or han held a considerable amount of autonomy, including the power to raise their own armies and impose taxes. It also involved replacing the Tokugawa military government that supposedly ruled in the name of a powerless emperor, and replacing it with a centralized Meiji government. Established in 1868, the new government adopted and adapted a wide range of Euro-American political, legal, military, and social institutions as it tried to re-make itself into a modern state of the Westphalian type.

Although the events of 1867-1868 are often referred to as the Meiji Restoration, suggesting a reversion to past ways at least in terms of imperial rule, this characterization is quite inaccurate. The processes in which the Tokugawa regime gave way to the Meiji government is best referred to as a Meiji Revolution, in which a feudal decentralized system was replaced by a unified sovereign state within which the central government took control over a single military force, introduced a national taxation system, and took direct charge of all foreign relations. These measures, as well as the establishment of a unified national education system, helped to give birth not just to a sovereign Japanese state, but in fact to a sovereign Japanese nation-state, in which the people were not merely subject to rule, but were also encouraged to see themselves as part of a national community of Japanese whose past was the history of the development of Japan, and whose present and future were tied to the fate of the Japanese state. As people in Japan came to understand themselves to be Japanese, they became more willing to act in the supposed interests of Japan.

The significance of this may be seen in the example of military service. In early Meiji Japan, when the Conscription Act was established, it was highly unpopular, and people around the Japanese islands rioted against what they termed a "blood tax". They did not see themselves as Japanese people who had an obligation to participate in guaranteeing the military security of the Japanese state. But three decades on, around the turn of the century, the situation had changed considerably. Largely due to the effects of national education and media, as well as conscription, people actively supported engagement in the Sino-Japanese and Russo-Japanese wars, and were, compared to before, much more willing to make sacrifices in the national interest. These international conflicts marked the emergence of popular nationalism and the successful mobilization of popular energies for external war.

In short, not only had Japan acquired the structural form of the modern state through institutional transformation, it had also acquired the subjective form of the modern state, or a nation, through the same processes. From a constructionist viewpoint, these developments reveal how understandings of statehood and the international order, as well as of Japan and what it means to be Japanese, are not natural and fixed, but fluid and developed in interaction. Because identities and rules associated with them are negotiated in relationships with others, the way they are is contingent or accidental, and it is likely that they will keep on mutating into the future. Next, we will consider what constructivist insights can bring when applied to the case of realist theories.

7-3 A constructivist perspective on realist thinking

Simply stated, realist theories suppose that the fact of state sovereignty produces an anarchic system. Self-interested states need to assure their own survival and independence in this anarchic system, engaging in self-help as far as possible, and allying with others only when absolutely necessary. States value security above all else, and because of this, they seek especially military and economic power. For realists, this statement at once presents an objective account of how the world is, and also provides guidelines about how to act in the world.

However, constructivists suggest that matters are not as simple as realists may believe. It is true that there may be no world government, and that anarchy may exist in the world system. But this does not mean that anarchy is necessarily risky, or that other states are necessarily dangerous. Anarchy only leads to self-help when interaction leads to the formation of identities and norms that position others as risks to guard against, rather than as possibilities for profit and mutual benefit. Although neo-realists may think that state identities and interests are clear and obvious, constructivists propose that in fact, interaction produces identities and interests that are constantly changing as a result of what actors do. Thus successful experiments in cooperation and mutual profit, as we suggested in the section on liberal institutionalism, may lead to an entirely different and more optimistic understanding of the possibilities of anarchy.

A well-known example used to illustrate the constructivist perspective concerns the end of the Cold War. Alexander Wendt argues that on the day that the Union of Soviet Socialist Republics and the

United States of America decided that they were no longer enemies, the Cold War was over. That is, when actors stopped thinking about themselves as fundamentally opposed, then they really were no longer opposed in their actions. The effect of the USSR and the USA interacting in new ways based on emerging new identities was nothing less than the transformation of the world system as a whole. This shift in identities led to the disappearance of the longstanding bipolar model, and caused a gradual move towards a unipolar model dominated by the United States, with both of these actors developing new expectations and understandings both of themselves, and of others, in their global interactions.

Using the constructivist approach to think about evolutions in world politics helps us to see that the way the world is today is the result of historical developments involving the dynamic interaction of various actors, whose understandings of self and the rules that bind them are affected by changing international and domestic conditions, and other actors. The important message that we should note from this is that it is highly likely that the future will be quite different from our present circumstances, that actors other than states may appear, that states may come to think about themselves in quite different ways, and that state interests and obligations may become quite different to the way that they currently are.

7-4 Debates concerning the constructivist approach

It is possible to criticize the constructivist approach on several major grounds. Firstly, there is an important issue concerning the question of how ideas and identities change. Constructivism argues that ideas and identities change, thus leading to different action in the state system, and sometimes to the creation of a new system. But why does such change occur?

Causation and meaning

The question of causation has not yet been fully addressed. Do material changes in the world—for example economic growth, or military buildup—lead actors to develop changed identities and act in different ways? Alternatively, does the process unfold the other way around, with ideas and identities shifting first? To uphold the former position suggests that ideas change the world less than the world changes ideas, while the second position leaves unanswered the question of why ideas and identities shift. This relationship between material conditions and subjective understandings is not satisfactorily explained by constructivist theories, critics say.

To this, the constructivist may answer that there is a dynamic relation between material transformations and shifts in identities and ideas. They may stress that the meaning of particular material transformations is not set but negotiated through interaction, and that this is what matters.

The post-World War II Western European states, for example, after two massive wars, began cooperating on a small scale in economic reconstruction and re-industrialization. Gradually, they expanded the range of their common activities to cover trade, finance, agriculture, human rights, and even defense. Although the conditions of anarchy were substantially the same—lack of government, self-interested states—what the European states made of them in the post-war era is quite different to what they made of them in the pre-war era. In that sense, we must suggest that there is at least some validity to the idea that identities and norms are not fixed. It seems possible that modifications in the way that people think about themselves and others may indeed lead to transformations in the way that people act, and that even if anarchy remains in place for some time to come, it may be anarchy with cooperation and mutual support as in the contemporary European Union, rather than anarchy with competition, distrust, and military conflict, as in early twentieth century Europe.

Explanation and prescription

This leads us to a second common criticism of constructivism, which is that it provides an explanation of how identities and associated norms make actors act the way they do, but does not give any particular guidance as to how actors should act. Neo-realism and liberalism, for example, try to explain the existing system and provide suggestions about how to act in the world. But constructivism seems not to be particularly influential in this respect: knowing that norms and identities are socially constructed helps us to see that they are not absolute, but created by humans, and so open to being changed. But this knowledge tells us little about desirable or less desirable actions for states.

Chapter 7 Constructivism in international relations theory

The meaning of anarchy

Lastly, neo-realists oppose the constructivist proposal that "anarchy is what states make of it". That is, this statement may be taken to suggest that state actors can choose to take on cooperative identities, and make an anarchic system characterized more by cooperation and friendship than competition and distrust.

This is certainly not impossible, as Costa Rica has shown. Article 12 of its 1949 Constitution abolished the Army, and stated that military forces "may only be organized under a continental agreement or for the national defense". Today, it has a lightly armed police force, but is fundamentally demilitarized. (Japan, of course, has a constitution that renounces war, but in fact the country is quite heavily militarized.) This fact affects how Costa Ricans think and act in the world, as a neutral disarmed state. As well, it influences how others think and act, towards Costa Rica. But at a wider level, the existence of a demilitarized state like Costa Rica suggests to others the possibility of another way of being and acting in the world, which may provide a model for more states to follow in the future.

However, neo-realists consider that this kind of subjective identity and action is not a possible choice for all states at all times, but is limited by material considerations to a very few specific cases. From the neo-realist viewpoint, what matters most is the fact that self-interested states exist in a state of international anarchy. Inadequate information, or even deceptive behavior by others, makes it impossible to be sure about the intentions of other states. Given these facts, even if it would be desirable for states to be cooperative and friendly, it is simply not possible for state leaders responsibly to choose demilitarization and cooperation. That is, holding a cooperative and friendly outlook in a risky world may appear to be simple weakness, and draw aggressive responses. Policy-makers have a responsibility to their publics to avoid this risk.

The constructivist reply to such concerns may be that neo-realists have a very restricted set of beliefs about the world, states, anarchy, and policy-making. Staying faithful to those beliefs seems likely to ensure the continuity of a world in which risk and suspicion remain strong, because of constant and widespread competitions over military strength and economic wealth. If constructivism can be said to lead to normative prescriptions, then one of them may be the suggestion that neo-realist determinism about the need for self-help to assure national independence and survival is one of the things that make the world system seem dangerous and risk-filled. For neo-realists to try to see the world through other lens, trying out other identities and perspectives, may well be an important step towards a more cooperative and friendly world. And for this to happen, more sustained conversations between different theoretical approaches, and especially the willingness to take other positions and identities and norms seriously, will be necessary.

N.M.

Chapter 7 Constructivism in international relations theory

Questions

1. Use the constructivist perspective to explain the difference between (1) A and B as friends, (2) A and B as a couple, and (3) A and B as a married couple, and (4) A and B as a divorced couple, referring to identities and norms / rules. Where do these identities and rules come from?

2. "What matters in the international system is not the distribution of power and resources, but the meanings that people give to the distribution of power and resources." Discuss with reference to the distinction between the world and the meanings that people give it. Consider also, how are these meanings created? Where do they come from?

3. "Anarchy is what states make of it". Discuss.

4. Identity and ideas are key to International Relations. Discuss.

5. How might realists and liberals take issue with or criticize constructivist theories?

Chapter 8 Feminist theories of international relations

"Representation of the world, like the world itself, is the work of men; they describe it from their own point of view, which they confuse with the absolute truth." Simone de Beauvoir

In 1949, the French philosopher Simone de Beauvoir famously said that, "one is not born a women, but rather, becomes one". What she meant was that human babies are born into the world. Then the societies in which those babies are born classify them into two groups, female and male, based on their primary sexual characteristics. Which group a baby is classified into is important, because people treat girls and boys differently. That is, people socialize their children somewhat separately, according to the dominant ideas in their society about what male or female members of that society should be like. This is not because boys and girls are essentially different, but rather because people perceive boys and girls to be different types of human beings.

The ways in which this treatment differs is constantly changing, as dominant ideas about what is appropriate for girls and boys, and for women and men, changes. The social meanings of "man" and "woman", or ideas about gender, are not static. Rather, they are dynamic and always shifting, as people's thinking shifts in response both to interaction with other people, and in response to changing political and economic conditions.

However, the difference itself continues to be re-established, in families, classrooms, workplaces, public spaces, and virtual environments. We can see the extent of this in the fact that women and men, as groups, show relatively significant differences in a wide range of areas, ranging from life trajectories, family and work responsibilities, economic and political power, social prestige, values, communication styles, and so on.

Simply put, children treated as girls and boys tend to develop into relatively different groups of adult women and adult men, as a result of sex-based differences in socialization, and this re-creates gendered societies all around the world. Beauvoir was trying to say that

100

women are not naturally feminine, and nor are men naturally masculine; we become (more or less) feminine women and masculine men in society, because other actors in society expect that of us.

At first glance, these ideas may seem to have little direct connection with theories about international relations. However, an expanding school of what has been termed feminist international relations theory has taken insights about gender socialization and its effects, and used them to propose problems with the dominant theories of realism and liberalism, as well as to propose new paths towards conflict resolution and politics, and even to outline different ways of conceptualizing international order. This section gives a brief review of some of these developments.

8-1 Looking at the world through a gendered lens

If we look at the world through a realist lens, then systemic anarchy may appear to be its most significant characteristic. It gives rise to a need for states to engage in self-help, since there is no authority to guarantee peace and security at the systemic level. Anarchy leads states to choose policies aimed at increasing economic and military power, which are vital to maintain autonomy and guarantee a state's continued existence. A further consequence of this is that within states, those seen to be the main actors in the quest for military security and economic wealth—namely, soldiers and people in paid work—enjoy greater prestige and respect than civilians and people who are not engaged in paid work.

If we change lenses and this time look at this same world through a liberal lens, then things may appear quite different. Namely, anarchy may seem less important, if we begin with the assumption that humans are rational and self-interested. From a liberal perspective, these two characteristics should allow people to realize that self-help and power maximization are not the best way to achieve peace and prosperity. Instead, relying on the fact that people are self-interested, liberalism proposes that individual actors will act to maximize their own economic self-interest in conditions of political, economic and social freedom, and that this will lead to economic specialization, with benefits in terms of efficiency and productivity gains. These, if combined with international trade, can lead to overall increases in economic wellbeing. The resulting economic interdependence,

101

supported by a framework of international institutions and increased transnational connections, should make people disinclined to engage in armed warfare. Thus political, social and economic freedom for individuals should bring people to achieve global peace and prosperity for all. In this liberal view of the world, self-interested actors who seek to maximize their own gains in a rational way take center stage, and in order for liberalism's vision to be realized, individual freedom needs to be guaranteed.

If we change lenses yet again, and this time look at the world through gendered lenses that focus on gaps and differences between men and women, then it is likely that we will notice different things about the world. We would surely find it particularly noteworthy that all around the world, political, military and corporate affairs are dominated by men.

A world dominated by men

In mid-2014, for example, women heads of state numbered between 6-8%, while women held around 20% of the world's parliamentary seats. In other words, over 90% of heads of state, and around 80% of national politicians in the world are men.

The global political gender imbalance is massive, but it is still smaller than the gender gap in corporate governance. There are only a handful of countries where women hold over 20% of corporate directorships (Sweden, Finland and the United Kingdom). Norway, with its progressive laws, is far ahead of any other state with 40%. The proportion of women on corporate directors' boards in most states is between 8~15%. Japan is dramatically behind other advanced states, with women directors at around 2% of the total.

When it comes to matters concerning military affairs and national security, women are likewise a small minority. In terms of ministries of defense, security, policing and military bureaucracy, female ministers are exceedingly few (eight in 2014: most women ministers are in fields such as welfare, education, and health), and non-elected intelligence, police, and military heads are almost entirely male. Looking at military personnel, around 15% of United States and Canadian soldiers are women, with 7% of US top ranks being held by women. China is estimated to have around 8% female forces, while the corresponding figure for Japan is about 6%. Highly militarized Israel is an outlier in this sense, as women make up over 30% of soldiers and over half of all officers, with few restrictions on combat positions. In most countries, military women are not only a small minority, but are also restricted to non-combat positions, and are most numerous in military medical care and administration. It hardly needs stating that few reach the top military ranks.

A masculine political agenda

Does it matter if women are largely absent from the core international relations fields of state policy-making and military national security, as well as from corporate leadership? The answer depends firstly on whether we consider that men and women are different or not. If we assume, as gender-related studies indicate, that women and men present considerable differences in the ways that they are socialized, and in the ways that they understand various issues, and in what they consider to be legitimate approaches to problem-solving, then it starts to become obvious that having a particular sex take charge of politics and economics and security, to the exclusion of the other, means that the perspectives of half of humanity are not well reflected in decision-making in these particular areas.

Unless we assume that the perspectives and understandings of women are unimportant, or are less important than those of men, this imbalance appears to be highly problematic. Namely, the fact that world politics, at least as the term is currently understood, is male-dominated points to a key problem: the basic concepts, concerns and agenda of related policy-making and research reveal a strong bias towards a masculine view of the world.

As hinted at in the previous sentence, there is a related and deeper issue to consider here about our conception of what world politics is about. In what sense is it true that women are missing from world politics, and especially security related issues, as well as from the global corporate scene? In what sense is this untrue? Perhaps the absence of women is partly due to the fact that there is a problem with the way that world politics and international security and the corporate scene are defined.

Different perspectives on security

Realist thinking begins with assumptions about the risks of anarchy in a system made up of sovereign states, and proposes that security of existence and continued autonomy can best be assured through the possession of sufficient military and economic power to deter aggressive action by others. Thus national security is conceptualized as being predominantly an inter-state issue involving military, economic, and political actors. But feminist thinking set at the level of real people's everyday lives might suggest a very different way of thinking about security.

Women living or working near military bases, for example in Japan, Korea and formerly in the Philippines, have long been victimized by elevated rates of sexual and other forms of violence by especially U.S. soldiers. Of course, U.S. soldiers do not just commit crimes against foreign women. The rates of sexual violence by American male soldiers against fellow American women soldiers are also exceedingly high, as are the rates of domestic violence crimes committed by U.S. soldiers and ex-soldiers against their partners. Additionally, ninety percent of contemporary war casualties are said to be civilians, mainly women and children, who also make up a majority of the population in the world's refugee camps.

If we take these facts into consideration, then it becomes possible to say that even as they are claimed to be necessary to protect citizens, especially women and children, state military security policies and organizations may have the opposite effect in the real world, where they may threaten and even destroy the security of especially women. If more women were involved in national security policy-making, then it seems likely that sexual and other violence by the supposed protectors of national security would receive more criticism, and stronger remedial action. Indeed, this kind of violence would itself be a core security issue, since the real lives of real people are being threatened and damaged.

Another related issue concerns the fact that male soldiers have often engaged in actions that deliberately raise the level of insecurity for many women and children, without drawing massive critical attention. For example, although the rules of war specifically forbid the targeting of civilian non-combatants, before and during the Second World War, Japanese forces committed huge numbers of sexual crimes against Chinese women, while German forces did the same against Russian women, and then in their turn, Russian forces committed massive sexual crimes against German women. More recently in the 1990s, the war in the former Yugoslavia was notorious for the high levels of sexual violence intentionally deployed by male soldiers against women civilians as a strategy of war, as was the war in Rwanda, while in the 2000s and beyond, the ongoing conflicts in the Congo and the Sudan have shown a similar tendency. Surely it would be less likely for military and governmental authorities to accept that sexual terrorism is an unavoidable part of war, or to perceive it to be a legitimate strategy of war, if more women were involved in decision-making.

Given the above, feminist international relations theory suggests that women (and children) are not absent from international security issues. They are simply unseen or considered relatively unimportant by the powerful men who dominate thinking about state security, and whose opinions count much more than those of victimized women and children.

The conventional definitions of security exclude these kinds of issues, largely because these definitions are decided by men, who find the insecurity of particular women to be less important than abstract ideas about anarchy, self-help, and achieving state military security against the military forces of other state actors that are likewise dominated by men.

Different perspectives on the economy

It seems possible to state that a similar situation exists in the case of international economics and trade. The main actors in the field of international economics and trade are often assumed to be governments and large multinational corporations. Defined like this, women are few in this field. Most executives of large companies are men, who tend to share similarly privileged family and educational backgrounds. However, the picture shifts if we consider that large multinational corporations often depend on using many women workers.

For example, the fashion industry is highly globalized, with design taking place in key centers such as New York, Milan, Paris and Tokyo, and the actual production taking place in countries with relatively cheap labor costs, including Bangladesh, China, India, Mexico, and Indonesia. In many of these countries, most of the workers in the factories are women, who are often relatively lowly paid and working in quite harsh conditions, with few opportunities for promotion and higher pay.

The international service industry is also highly globalized, with call centers and data processing, for example, often outsourced from high-income countries to countries with cheaper labor costs, including India, China, and Sri Lanka. Such work too, tends to be done more by women than by men, and to be relatively low paid with restricted opportunities for promotion.

If we take these points into consideration, then it is clear that women are integral players in the global economy. However, they tend to be marginalized, in that men dominate the best paid, most powerful and desirable jobs, while women tend to have lower paid and less desirable jobs.

The economic marginalization of women is not a tendency found in only developing countries. In many developed countries too, an examination of paid economic activity reveals that the best paid and most powerful positions are dominated by men, while the most insecure and poorly paid positions are dominated by women.

Visibility and power

If we focus on high-level decision-making, and on corporate and government policy, women are not very visible. But a grassroots examination suggests to us that this lack of visibility may be related to their peripheral position in the paid economy. If we focus on the grassroots level where many women are mobilized for paid work, our definition of international economics may change, and lead us to focus more on gendered economic disparities both within and between countries.

A further point to consider is that economics is often treated as the domain of paid "productive" work, with "reproductive" work—including paid and unpaid childcare work, housework, and aged care work—treated as marginal or non-core activities. This unpaid work, done overwhelmingly by women, in fact is the basis of all other kinds of work, and also one of the major conditions that limits women's participation in paid work. Predominantly male soldiers can go to war because their largely female partners undertake domestic duties and look after children. Largely male corporate employees can devote themselves to their work because their often female partners take on childcare and aged care duties. Although reproductive labor is arguably more important than any other kind of work, it receives little if any pay, minimal recognition, and is overwhelmingly the responsibility of women.

Like men, women play indispensable economic roles all around the world. However, compared to men, their roles tend not to receive equal recognition, suffering from low pay, lack of decision-making power, and even no pay.

Overall, use of a gendered lens to examine world politics suggests that it may be necessary to redefine international security and economics so that they become sensitive to gender-related inequalities and blind-spots. It may also be desirable to seek changes in the composition of decision-makers, and to promote changes in the way that policy decisions are made.

8-2 Feminist critiques of realism

Feminist theorists propose that the fact that international relations has been dominated by men, both in terms of academic theories, and in terms of practice by politicians, bureaucrats and soldiers, is highly significant. This is because in most societies, compared to the way women are socialized, there is a tendency for men to be encouraged to be more competitive; to see contests in terms of winning and losing; and to value independence and autonomy more than dependence and cooperation. Also, in almost all societies, male physical violence is more tolerated than female physical violence.

Many feminists say that the effects of these tendencies can be seen in classical theories of realism and in neoclassical theories of realism. The former, for example, is based on a view of others as rivals and threats, who are to be deterred from attacking primarily by brute force. The latter is based on a conception of anarchy in which others are always potential threats, and advises us to assure our security by engaging in self-help so that we can be as strong as possible. This is because, realist thinking commonly claims, mutual dependence and trust are too dangerous or too risky, for states that exist in an anarchic system.

Cooperation as natural

A theory like this could only have been thought of by men, some feminists argue. This is because for women, society and others cannot be perceived primarily as threats and rivals.

For women, who require the assistance of others around them especially in the times just before and after giving birth, others are people to depend on in cooperative relationships. For women who as primary care-givers tend to have children and elderly people depend heavily on them, society is not essentially competitive, and others are not obvious threats.

The vital work of sustaining and reproducing human life has been in many societies delegated primarily to women, and women's engagement in such work is based on mutual dependence and trust, rather than mutual suspicion and high levels of armament. It is from this perspective that the realist worldview and recommendations about action appear to reflect a particular masculine view of the world.

Interdependence and mutual trust are in fact integral parts of the human condition not just for women, children and aged people, but all people at all stages of life, and for all states in today's integrated global socio-economic and political system. In terms of socio-economic relations, for example, no-one is able to live and thrive on their own, with any real level of autonomy or independence. Realism can thus be criticized as seeking to reject something that is intuitively an unavoidable fact of life. The masculine realist insistence that people and states should seek independence and autonomy is, from this perspective, an impossible dream.

Against cultures of militarism

Feminists also draw connections between realism's insistence that military and economic power is the most important solution to living in anarchy and dealing with international disputes, and dominant forms of masculinity. In many countries, boys are socialized into a military culture in a way that girls are not. Giving tanks, rockets, rifles and other kinds of military-themed "toys" and "games" to male children is likely to be considered relatively unproblematic or even normal. By comparison, giving such "toys" to female children is likely to meet with a strong negative reaction. Popular culture is full of stories in which male heroes use physical and military strength to resolve conflicts and make the world safe. In such stories, and in the schoolyard, for a boy to back down in a dispute and accept a compromise in the schoolyard, rather than to fight in assertion of his position, is more likely to lead to accusations of weakness, or of being like a girl, than it is to positive evaluation of his peace-loving character.

Societies in which boys are brought up to see military weapons as something close to them and valuable, and in which boys are raised on stories about men legitimately using armed force in order to establish or restore justice, and in which they are encouraged to use force rather than compromise or negotiate are, say feminists, societies in which men, much more than women, are going to consider violence a legitimate means of communication, in both their everyday lives and in international relations. Having decision-makers who are overwhelmingly male may be considered to be unwise, at least from the perspective of minimizing the risk of armed conflict around the world.

8-3 Feminist critiques of liberal theories

Just as realist theories can be criticized for privileging a particularly masculine worldview and set of values, so too can liberalism. Feminist theories of international relations take issue especially with the nature of human rationality as it is assumed by liberal theories.

Among the core assumptions of liberal thinking is the idea that humans are rational and self-interested individuals. In economics, for example, humans are said to calculate how they can maximize their own profits, and to act accordingly. As humans seek to act according to their self-interest, they specialize in particular activities that offer them the best returns. As all people do this, the end result is a complex division of labor. This leads to increased overall well-being, as economic specialization leads to increased efficiency and productivity. It also leads to a decreased chance of conflict, since economic actors are also forced to trade with others in order to obtain the goods and services that they do not produce for themselves. Increases in economic wealth and interdependence, especially if they occur across state borders, are seen to be major factors that can help lead to a reduction in armed conflict.

Against economic rationality

However, liberalism assumes that this type of economic rationality is characteristic of human beings, when in fact, in the real world, it has historically been more characteristic of men. Men in modern labor markets situated within capitalist societies have tended to act according to these principles of rational self-interest.

However, this idea would seem ridiculous in non-capitalist subsistence societies where the pursuit of increased material wealth is

109

not assumed to be a primary human goal. It also appears counter-intuitive in the case of people who choose to have children and so to incur great costs in terms of time and lost work hours, or to work for their communities or for the public sector at lower salaries than are available in the private sector, or to engage in nursing and childcare and other forms of care work where salaries are low in comparison to the heavy burden required.

People do not necessarily seek to maximize their profits, it seems. Indeed, self-interested rationality, from this perspective, seems like something that people need to be socialized into having, rather than being a natural part of human psychology.

If especially many women work as lower-paid teachers, nurses, and social workers, and if especially many women undertake domestic work, childcare work and aged care work even without receiving salaries, then this suggests that liberal claims about rational self-interest and profit maximization do not apply to these many women. Liberal theories that assume humans are self-interested rational actors, then, only partially explain the economic behavior of only some social actors.

From this perspective, liberalism obviously cannot be a universal model. It seems rather to be only a partial model that applies mainly to men in capitalist economies marked by a division of labour between men who are concentrated in the middle and upper reaches of the paid economy, and women who are concentrated in the unpaid economy and the lower reaches of the paid economy.

Free trade and gender

Liberal theories also propose that free trade is desirable because it leads to overall increases in wealth. Realists are less keen on completely free trade because the benefits tend to be unevenly distributed between states, and some states are likely to benefit more than others. Feminists, however, point out that the benefits of free trade may not just be unevenly distributed between states, but also between men and women within and between states.

In particular, the profits from free trade tend to go disproportionately towards investors and large corporations, rather than to grassroots workers. The relative concentration of men among the ranks of investors and large corporation boards, and the relative concentration of women in export industries such as garment production and call centers, means that free trade's benefits tend to go more to men than to women. Thus the effect of free trade can be to worsen the economic gap between men and women, even as it brings about overall increases in economic prosperity.

Democracy and gender

Finally, liberal theories also propose that democracy and international institutions are desirable, because they provide peaceful guidelines for conflict resolution, as well as sites for states to negotiate over common problems and issues. This is certainly true. However, some feminists would claim that democracy in male-dominated societies does not work well to solve the problems of gender inequality. Because such societies are characterized by male-centric values and norms, the political agenda often does not deal with women's interests equally to men's interests. The dominance of politics by men even in wealthy and progressive liberal democratic states may be considered to support this criticism. Furthermore, the dominance of men in domestic politics tends to spill-over into the dominance of men in international politics too.

Using a gendered lens to examine our everyday politics, economies, and societies thus leads us to perceive a rather different world, where inequalities of power and economic resources are problems not just between states, but also problems for women and men, both within and between states. Part of the problem lies in actual material conditions, where men dominate powerful positions in politics and the economy, while women are relatively more common in less powerful or even marginal positions in politics, the economy, and the home. But part of the problem also lies in the way that we think about and define important domains. Defining international relations in a limited way can work to exclude women from international relations. Making a more inclusive academic discipline of international relations may help us to imagine a world with very different arrangements for politics, economy, and society.

N.M.

Questions

1. What does it mean to say that gender is a social construction?

2. International and national policy-making has been dominated by men. How significant is this for understanding global politics?

3. Why is the myth that wars are fought to protect women and children problematic from a feminist perspective? How might feminists approach the understanding of state violence?

4. Why do some feminists believe that national security may be bad for individual security? What is your view on this claim?

5. How and why does the gendered division of labor contribute to women's subordination relative to men? How does it contribute to men's relative success?

6. How might gender-sensitive lenses consider other theories about international relations in other chapters?

7. How might realists and liberals see feminist theories of international relations?

Chapter 9 Foreign policy and state actors

"Nations do not distrust each other because they are armed. They are armed because they distrust each other." Ronald Reagan

When states make decisions, the potential consequences for citizens are huge. Changes in policies related to tax levels, welfare payments or the provision of public services have a significant and direct impact on the population. This is, of course, the reason why, in democracies, people vote. Citizens vote for the political party that they think will best meet their needs. However, while domestic policies are important for the study of international relations, we are really interested in foreign policies.

The potential consequences for citizens of a state's foreign policies are also huge. Looking at one extreme example, if a state pursues a course of war, then some citizens will be required to sacrifice their freedom and possibly even their lives in the pursuit of this policy objective. The citizens will have no choice in this matter. The state is able to use its monopoly on the use of power to force its citizens to fight.

Foreign policies towards particular states have the potential to affect all spheres of the bilateral relationship. For example, a foreign policy to build and enhance a security alliance will almost certainly enhance political relations, but will likely also result in an expansion of social and economic interactions. Likewise a foreign policy to target market access, will have an impact on other aspects of the bilateral economic relationship. In this way, foreign policies in one area will have spillover effects in other areas. Indeed, we must assume that the great range of potential effects is considered in the process of formulating foreign policy.

We can therefore see that foreign policies will have a considerable effect on citizens. For example, citizens of friendly states typically enjoy preferential visa and immigration rules, meaning that it is easier to travel to countries which are friendly with one's own. Japanese citizens, for example, have preferential access to those countries with which Japan has strong economic relations, such as the US or EU member states. This ease of personal travel is a necessary component of the intensified interactions, another component of which is the ease of trade.

Another example concerns natural resources. Foreign policies often target access to natural resources such as oil and gas, and the success or failure of such policies will invariably affect the domestic price of such natural resources. Alternatively, a foreign policy may target access to overseas markets for domestically produced goods. This will affect the ability of domestic producers to export, which will in turn impact domestic employment.

In this chapter, we will look at how foreign policy is made. To so this, we will utilize the three levels of analysis that were introduced earlier. We will first look at the systemic influences on foreign policy. These are the international factors that affect foreign policy decision-making. Following on from this, we will investigate the domestic influences on foreign policy. Finally, we will look at individual factors that influence foreign policy.

When we talk about foreign policy, we must identify which officials are involved in the decision making process, and the goals of the particular foreign policy as well as the values that underpin these goals. We must also consider the tools or instruments that affect the ability of the state to pursue different foreign policies.

9-1 System level factors affecting foreign policy making

The international environment is obviously important to the formulation of foreign policy. Foreign policy is a states' response to the international situation at that time. In this way, the international environment provides a set of opportunities and constraints for foreign policy.

The distribution of power within the international environment is important, as is the web of relations around the most powerful states. Furthermore, the geographic position of the state relative to the most powerful states is also important.

Polarity

Polarity is a term used to describe the distribution of power between and among states. Unipolarity is a situation in which power is

Chapter 9 Foreign policy and state actors

overwhelmingly concentrated in the hands of one state. It is often said that this was the situation that arose after the end of the Cold War, when America had its "unipolar moment". With the collapse of the Soviet Union, no other state could come close to matching America's power. America had vast superiority in military power, economic power, political power, and social/cultural "soft power".

Because of the rise of China and other regional powers, some have argued that this period of unipolarity is either over or now ending. It is obvious that such a change in the international environment will dramatically affect the formulation of foreign policy by all states. Today, states such as Japan or Britain, that are very close allies of America, always have to carefully consider the likely response of America to any foreign policy that they may make. This means that America exerts great influence over the formulation of foreign policy within these states. Alternatively, states such as North Korea may make virtually all foreign policy decisions in light of their expected response from America. Conversely, the opposite is rarely true. America may make some policy-decisions, giving full consideration to the possible reactions of other actors. But the superpower in unipolar conditions is more likely to put its own interests first, and to consider the possible reactions of others second.

Bipolarity is an international environment in which power is concentrated in two states. The best example we have of this is the Cold War, in which the USA and the USSR had comparable military power. Indeed one of the most important characteristics of the Cold War was the perpetual arms race, which saw both sides strive for superiority in weapons and technology. Whilst arms races are extremely dangerous for the preservation of international peace, during the Cold War, it could be considered that there existed a balance of power between the two superpowers which preserved peace (or at least prevented the outbreak of World War Three).

Needless to say, during the Cold War, states had to carefully consider their position within the bipolar world when making foreign policy decisions. Indeed, because of the potential danger to newly independent postcolonial states in this bipolar world, many smaller states pursued neutral or non-aligned foreign policies.

Because of the enormous numbers of nuclear weapons that each of the superpowers possessed during the Cold War, a situation of

Mutually Assured Destruction (MAD) developed in which it became impossible for the USA and USSR to engage in direct military conflict, as it would have resulted in the destruction of mankind. This meant that both superpowers competed in the arena of world opinion (for example, the Space Race and the Olympic Games), whilst also trying to maximize their own power and influence while limiting the others'.

This meant that the Cold War was often fought in the newly independent countries of the 'Third World'. Conflict such as the Korean War and the Vietnam War can only be understood within the framework of the bipolarity of the Cold War. As a result of this, large number of smaller states joined the 'non-aligned movement' aimed at maintaining neutrality in the Cold War. Countries such as India, Burma and Indonesia were important for the formation of this movement. For these states, the bipolar international environment was possibly the key factor influencing their foreign policies.

A multipolar world is one in which power is concentrated in a few states. There are more than two centers of power in the international environment. It may be that we are now entering into a period of multipolarity, although we usually use the period from the 19th century leading up to the outbreak of World War One as an example of a multipolar world. Whilst during the 19th century Britain was the predominant power, its power relative to other states was beginning to fall by the end of the 19th century. By the beginning of the 20th century, Germany was unified and becoming an economic and military powerhouse. This was worrying for the other European Great Powers of France, Russia and Britain. Across the Atlantic Ocean, America was also emerging as an economic force, as was Japan in East Asia. We therefore had a period in which there were a multitude of centers of power. This situation proved to be highly unstable, and competition between the European Great Powers directly led to the outbreak of World War One, or the Great War.

Polarization

It was the system of alliances between the European Great Powers, and between the Great Powers and smaller states, which ultimately dragged all of Europe into the Great War. In all different types of polarity, there exists a network of alliances that bind states to each other.

The degree to which states cluster around the center, or centers,

Chapter 9 Foreign policy and state actors

of power is called polarization. For example, during the bipolar Cold War, there was a group of states that clustered around the USA. In Europe, these states formed a group called the North Atlantic Treaty Organization (NATO). But, Australia, Canada, Japan, South Korea, Taiwan and a host of other states also formed alliances with America. On the other side, Central and Eastern European states formalized their alliance with the Soviet Union through the Warsaw Pact Treaty. Furthermore, Cuba, North Korea, Vietnam and a host of other states also formed alliance with the USSR. Thus, during the Cold War, we had a web of alliances that tied many states to one of the two centers of power in that bipolar world. Needless to say, when a state depends on another state for their security, it must carefully consider that state's response in all foreign policy decisions. In this way more powerful states can influence the foreign policy of smaller, less powerful states.

Finally, there is a nonpolar distribution of power in the world environment. Under conditions of nonpolarity, there are no centers of power. No state has overwhelming power, and instead power is diffused, dispersed across many states, as well as non-state actors, such as international organizations and non-government organizations. Some have argued that the 21st century will be characterized by unipolarity, and this will be discussed in the later section on non-state actors.

Geopolitics

A state's geographical position has a very significant influence on its foreign policy. Whether or not the state is an island nation or a continental one, whether the state has sea borders or mountain borders, and who the state's neighbors are will all be important factors for decision makers to consider when making foreign policy.

If we look at the United States, we can easily see the importance of geographical factors. The USA is separated from Europe and Asia by vast oceans which provide a natural defense, because such oceans are relatively difficult to cross. Furthermore, the USA has never had neighbors that could become an enemy potentially strong enough to threaten it. Therefore, the USA has enjoyed a relatively safe position in the world, which allowed it to industrialize and develop without the threat of invasion. This in turn has allowed the USA to pursue an isolationist foreign policy for much of its history.

Such an option is not available to many states. Germany for example, is at the very center of Europe. It is surrounded by other states,

117

and for much of its history these states have been perceived to be threats to Germany's security. Under such conditions, isolationism is not a policy option. In the 21st century, Germany's foreign policy is dictated by its position as a central player in the European Union.

Britain's position as an island nation just off the European continent has long been an important factor in the formulation of its foreign policy. As an island nation, Britain developed a strong navy several centuries ago to protect its overseas trade routes, and this later underpinned its empire. Preserving this sea border has long been a priority of Britain's foreign policy, and this perspective helps to explain Britain's current reluctance to accept full integration with the European Union.

Japan's position as an island nation allowed it to follow an extreme isolationist foreign policy in the Tokugawa period. The Japanese government, prior to the arrival of Commander Perry's black ships, attempted to close its borders to almost all foreign influence. Whilst there was a steady trickle of foreigners arriving and settling in Japan during this time, the official government policy was to close off Japan from the world. Furthermore, Japan's geographical position as an island nation neighboring China has always had been an important factor for Japan's foreign policy. Indeed, competition and conflict with the USA over access to the China market was an important factor behind the outbreak of the Pacific War.

Thus, these geopolitical factors have long been considered to be essential for understanding the formulation of a state's foreign policy. Geographical location and geographical features shape leader's perceptions of the options available to them in their decision making process.

So, the distribution of power in the international system and the web of alliances around the centers of power, as well as geopolitical factors are international factors that influence foreign policy. These factors are located at the system level of analysis. Let us now turn to the state level of analysis and look at domestic influences on foreign policy.

9-2 State Level Factors affecting foreign policy making

Whereas the system level factors provide constraints and opportunities for a state, the domestic situation in the state itself will

Chapter 9 Foreign policy and state actors

determine the ability of the state to take action. There are a vast number of domestic factors that affect the capacity of a state to make and then effectively implement foreign policy. However, for the purpose of simplicity, we will divide these into the following categories; level of economic development, military capabilities, type of government, and institutional factors.

Level of economic development

A country's level of economic development has a direct and defining influence on its foreign policy. Indeed, the level of economic development will determine to a great degree the capacity of the state to carry out its foreign affairs.

Generally, states at more advanced levels of economic development are more active internationally, which means that they have more comprehensive foreign policy agendas. There is a very simple reason for this. The currently dominant model of economic development is built on industrialization and trade, and this means that as a country develops, it becomes steadily more integrated into the global economy. An example of this could be the domestic need for certain resources that are to be found only in a small number of places, such as rare earth metals that are essential for the manufacture of high-technology consumer products, such as mobile phones. The domestic demand for the resource provides the foreign policy imperative.

As a country develops economically, therefore, its foreign affairs become broader and more complex, and this means the state becomes more interested in issues that are not domestic issues. States at higher levels of economic development also have greater technological capabilities which influence foreign policy. It is natural to assume that more economically advanced states should have more capabilities in general than less economically advanced states, and this should translate into more effective foreign policy. Economically advanced countries should have higher productivity, as well as higher technical capabilities.

Conversely, states at lower levels of economic development are assumed to generally have lower capabilities in carrying out effective foreign policy. Furthermore, their dependence on capital and technology from the richer states limits their ability to formulate independent foreign policy. However, having said that, there are cases whereby less economically developed states are able to use the rich

119

state's dependence on certain natural resources to improve their negotiating position. A good example of this is the oil-rich, but often economically less developed OPEC states, which have been able to exploit the dependence of rich states on fossil fuels to improve their position.

It is also generally the case that economically advanced rich states tend to want to preserve the status quo. This means they want to keep the international system in its current form. It is indeed natural that such states would act in such a way. Such economically successful states have benefited from the way the international system is organized, and would perceive that system to be a good one. Conversely, less economically advanced states will likely view the international system in exactly the opposite way. They may perceive the international system to be restricting its ability to develop; to be constraining it, precisely because they are less developed. More importantly perhaps, a rising power, a state that is developing economically may benefit from the international system as it is, while also seeking to reform certain important aspects of it.

We should be careful not to generalize about the importance of the level of economic development to a states' foreign policy. There are a multitude of other factors that are also important. It may be best to say that the level of development affects leaders' perceptions of the capacity of the state, as well as perceptions of the opportunities and constraints. Needless to say, the level of economic development directly affects a states' military capability, to which we turn next.

Military capability

States spend considerable time and resources on preparing for war. War games and military exercises are designed to prepare the military for different types of conflict, but also more importantly perhaps, they are an opportunity for the state to show that they are preparing for war. This use of military force as a deterrence is an extremely useful foreign policy tool. Such war games are certainly less costly than the pursuit of war itself. The joint US- Republic of Korea military exercises are partly designed to deter the North Koreans from attacking.

Countries such as France and Britain have made the conscious choice that maintaining a strong military is a necessary component of their state's foreign policies. Both states maintain military capabilities

Chapter 9 Foreign policy and state actors

(nuclear submarines, aircraft carriers, etc.) that allow them to project their military power far beyond their nations' borders. This is presumably based on the assumption that it improves their ability to conduct effective foreign policy. Both states also maintain a nuclear weapons capability, although it is likely that this has more to do with the preservation of status. In the current international environment, it is difficult to image a situation in which France or Britain would use their nuclear weapons.

In response to China's aggressive moves in relation to the small group of rocks called the Senkaku or Diaoyu Islands, the Japanese government has been building up its military capabilities. This is despite US assurances that the islands are covered by the US-Japan security alliance. This is further evidence of the importance states place on military capabilities.

Another example comes from the Middle Eastern region. With the assistance of a number of Western powers, Iraqi dictator Saddam Hussein built up the military. With this strong military, Saddam Hussein then made the foreign policy decision to invade Kuwait in an attempt to control its oil. Saddam Hussein pursued military capability in order to increase his foreign policy choices. Conversely, the perception of overwhelming US military power in 2002 provided the Bush administration with the capability to pursue the foreign policy of regime change in Iraq. Importantly perhaps, it may have been this assumption of overwhelming military superiority that caused the planning for war to be prioritized at the expense of the planning for peace.

We can see therefore that military power is a key domestic influence on foreign policy. A state's level of military capabilities will influence the range of foreign policy options available to leaders. However, having said that, it may well be that perceptions of overwhelming military capability will cause an over-reliance on such foreign policy choices. This means that the state may choose a military option even when it is not the most optimal foreign policy choice. Needless to say, the potential consequences of such a scenario are considerable and largely negative. It is important to understand though, that there are different types of military capabilities, and these different types can only be effectively used in certain different situations. A very good example of this is that the United States' massive nuclear arsenal was ineffective at deterring the 9-11 terrorist attacks. Likewise, overwhelming US firepower was no match for the will of the North Vietnamese for independence and national unity during the Vietnam War.

At the state level of analysis it is necessary to consider military capabilities when attempting to understand foreign policy formulation. But, it is just one state level factor. Another important such factor is the type of government.

Types of government

A state's political system will invariably have an impact on its foreign policy. Different political systems have different decision-making processes. For the sake of simplicity, we will divide political systems into two types: democratic and autocratic. Democratic means some type of constitutional democracy or representative government, in which citizens choose their leaders through elections. Autocratic means authoritarian or totalitarian government, in which political power is held by a very small minority, and citizens cannot choose their leaders. Of course, some democratic states are more democratic than others, and likewise, some autocratic states are more autocratic than others.

In both types of political systems, leaders need support from some groups within their societies. In democratic states that have elections, leaders will need the support of a majority of the citizens in order to get elected. However, in autocratic states too, leaders will need support from certain groups, for examples, business elites, or the military.

An important difference is that in 'open' democratic societies, there is a public debate on most policy choices. This means that the mass media, the government and relevant interest groups carry out a public debate, the result of which will lead to policy. This pluralism is, at least in theory, one of the strong points of democratic government. The more opinions that are incorporated into the decision-making process, the better the final decision should be, and the more legitimacy that decision should have. Even opponents of a decision are likely to accept it as legitimate if they have been involved in the decision-making process.

However, in 'closed' autocratic states, decisions are made by a small group of elites who will have very similar interests and perspectives. In such a situation, it is likely that their decisions will reflect their narrow interests and positions.

Having said that, autocratic states generally are able to make decisions much faster than democratic states can. Democracies have so many different interest groups that the public debate on policy can take quite some time. It could also be the case that the small group of elites in an autocratic state could focus on the foreign policy issue itself. It may not need to consider the impact on certain domestic groups. In a democracy however, the domestic situation determines the environment in which the decision is made. Regardless of the foreign policy issue, even if it were a crisis that requires an immediate policy change, in a democracy, there must be at least some level of public debate.

Both democracies and autocracies may sometimes engage in what is called the diversionary theory of war. A state will pursue a certain foreign policy choice so as to distract the citizens from other domestic worries, such as serious economic problems. Leaders hope that they can appeal to nationalist tendencies in the population by engaging in a conflict or dispute with some 'other' unpopular actor.

With the dramatic spread of democracy through the 20th century, some scholars have suggested that the 21st century may benefit from democratic peace. This is the idea, based on the work of Immanuel Kant, whereby democracies are less likely to engage in war. Kant stated that, in democracies, because leaders have to listen to their citizens, and because citizens will have to fight and pay for the war, democratic leaders will be less likely to pursue aggressive foreign policies, particularly against other democracies. It seems likely that liberal democracies are indeed less likely to engage in war with each other. Certainly, if we look at Europe in the 21st century, the idea of these democracies fighting in a war is very difficult to imagine.

However, there is a danger here. If we believe that democracies are in general more peaceful, then it is in the interests of democratic states to try to spread democracy to non-democratic states. Certainly most democracies do indeed try to encourage democracy overseas, through their foreign aid programs, for example. But, the recent case of the US-led war against Iraq showed how democracies could engage in a war of aggression against an autocratic state, so as to make it into a democracy.

Institutional Factors

States are like complex machines. They have very many parts performing different functions. Like all large institutions, there are different parts that specialize in different things. This specialization should increase efficiency and productivity, as is also the purpose in economics. Leaders must use this variety of state institutions when making foreign policy decisions.

Even though realism assumes the state to be a unitary actor, we know that in reality, that is not the case. Within any state there are a multitude of actors in a multitude of government departments and agencies that may be involved in decision making processes.

Even if we assume that each official in each institution is working for the best interests of the state, it is probable that different officials in different parts of the government have different ideas about what is in the best interests of the state. Further, each government department or agency has a different focus. The Ministry of Foreign Affairs focuses on the foreign affairs, or international relations of that state, the Ministry of Trade and Industry focuses on that state's economy, the Ministry of Defense focuses on national security, narrowly defined as defense.

The focus, or specialization of each government department means that officials within that department naturally prioritize those issues that are related to the focus of their home department. This means that each official's idea of what is in the state's best interests will be partly determined by their department.

From the above, we can see that in the study of foreign policy formulation, it is not possible to see the state as a unitary actor. This becomes even more obvious when we consider the bureaucratic politics of any state.

In bureaucratic politics, policy is a result of negotiation and compromise between different government departments and agencies. The different parts of the government promote their own interests and attempt to maximize their own power. This means that officials understand their department's best interests to be the state's best interests. Different departments compete over budgets and staffing. Departments fight for survival in a competitive arena, and it is this that becomes the priority for officials. Of course, bureaucratic politics does

Chapter 9 Foreign policy and state actors

not mean that policy is decided with no consideration of the issue with which it is related, although unfortunately this may happen. It merely means that the interests of different state institutions must also be taken into consideration when trying to understand the decision making process.

Bureaucratic politics is one factor which undermines rational choice. Rational choice theory says that decisions are made by carefully considering all aspects of a problem in search of the best solution. According to this idea, decision makers clearly define their goals, assess the potential costs and benefits of each policy choice and its potential outcomes, and then make the best or optimal choice.

However, in the real world, such a process is probably impossible. Bureaucratic politics restricts the ability of officials to make decisions in line with rational choice. However, more importantly perhaps, decision makers will never have complete information about the problem which enables them to make the rational choice. It is not possible for officials to have all the information on all the potential outcomes of all the different policy choices. Furthermore, decisions are often made under time pressures. This means that there is often insufficient time to carefully consider all the potential outcomes, all the potential costs and benefits. This means that decisions are always made with insufficient information to make the rational choice.

The previous section outlines how bureaucratic politics is one problem of institutions. However, because of their complexity, institutions also have standard operating procedures, which guide officials in their everyday work. This means that officials are trained to follow the standard operating procedures when they deal with problems or issues that arise. Such a system can, and often does, become inflexible, limiting innovation. It is likely that this causes institutions to change only very slowly, and will also limit their ability to respond effectively to new issues.

It seems that the combination of bureaucratic politics and standard operating procedures can make bureaucracies very inefficient, even ineffectual. A good example of this is provided by the case of the 9-11 terrorist attacks on America. Even though a number of government agencies had received warnings about upcoming terrorist attacks involving hijacked airliners, no action was taken. It is now generally accepted that one of the main reasons for the lack of action was that different government departments and agencies were not sharing the information they had. If they had shared the information, it is likely that someone would have seen the danger. Even though all these departments and agencies have the same purpose (national security), they are unlikely to cooperate and likely to try to protect their own interests.

Furthermore, emotions may also limit the ability of leaders to make the best decisions. For example, a leader may make a decision when angry or frustrated. Policy inertia, a situation in which policy does not change even when conditions change dramatically, may result from bureaucratic inertia, but may also result from the emotional attachment of a leader to his/her policy. The leader does not want to admit that their policy is not working, and so resists change.

In addition to these restrictions on individual rational choice, there are also a number of ways in which groups of decision makers may also not work effectively. Groupthink is a situation in which the social pressures of the group cause people to conform to the majority position. While such groups are intended to use a range of different voices to 'brainstorm', and generate the best possible policy option, the opposite may be the case. Individuals act for group harmony, rather than for the best policy. Newly-formed groups may also suffer from Newgroup Syndrome whereby members are unfamiliar with each other and with the procedures of the group and so act in a conservative manner.

So, we have examined the four main domestic influences on foreign policy; level of economic development, military capabilities, type of government and institutional factors.

We have already discussed how domestic factors affect foreign policy. However, according to Robert Putnam's two-level games theory, leaders play two games at the same time. One game is at the international level, which involves foreign policy, and the other game is at the domestic level. A decision on one level will affect the other level. Indeed, leaders must consider the both of the two levels. Smart leaders will seemingly play on one level, but will in fact be playing on both levels at the same time. Of course, from this viewpoint, it is difficult to separate the two levels, and this may be a more suitable model of reality. Foreign and domestic policies, international and national politics, are difficult to separate.

Chapter 9 Foreign policy and state actors

9-3 Individual Level Factors in foreign policy making

When we look at foreign policy using the individual level of analysis, we are looking at the willingness and ability of leaders to take action when they have the opportunity. We have shown how both the international environment and the domestic situation are both important for foreign policy, no analysis is complete without a look at the leaders who are actually making the decisions. So, we will next investigate the personal characteristics of leaders.

It should of course be the case that only the best and brightest people become our leaders. Whilst ambition is essential, we expect our leaders to be smart and persuasive. The best leaders are also very charismatic, and this is one of the sources of their authority. Leaders also get authority from the positions they hold in government, military, the bureaucracy, and so on. Leaders must be great communicators, but they must also be able to analyze information effectively, and they must be able to persuade people to do things, even if they don't want to.

It is important too that leaders have political efficacy, which means having the confidence of others in their ability to lead and successfully manage what happens. Leaders must believe that they are able to control the decision making process.

Whilst leaders are expected to be able to act rationally, to make decisions according to reason, we know that this is not so simple. Leaders depend on their bureaucracies for the information that is necessary for them to make a rational decision, and that information will never be complete. Despite this, the leader must be able to use the information available to make the best possible decision.

We have already discussed ways in which leaders are not able to make decisions according to rational choice. The incomplete information available as well as the often limited time available result in a situation whereby leaders choose the most satisfactory policy option, and not the optimal or best policy option. This is called satisficing. The satisfactory option may only meet minimal standards, but leaders pressed for time and lacking information tend to choose this option rather than spending more time on finding a better option.

Another constraint on rational decision-making is proposed by prospect theory, which says that leaders fear potential losses more than they value potential gains. This means that a leader is more likely to

127

follow a risky policy so as to minimize losses than to maximize gains.

These points suggest that there are a number of serious constraints on the foreign policy decision-making process. In an ideal world, all decisions are made according to rational choice, whereby leaders have all the information they need to make a decision, and fully consider all the potential costs and benefits of each policy choice. In reality however, information is never complete and time is limited. On top of this, the various psychological factors can affect rational choice too. Furthermore, different government bureaucracies may not be cooperating and may in fact be working against each other.

Having said all that, for the study of international relations, it is necessary to attempt to understand how and why foreign policies are made. To help in our understanding of this, we can use the three levels of analysis outlined earlier in this book.

P.S.

Questions

1. In what ways is a state's geographical position important for its foreign policy?
2. Many state's sovereignty is now under threat. Discuss.
3. Explain and discuss the organizational constraints on effective foreign policy formulation.
4. Explain the bureaucratic politics model, and discuss how it affects foreign policy formulation.
5. Explain the importance of polarity for foreign policy making.

Chapter 10 Non-state actors in world politics

"More than ever before in human history, we share a common destiny. We can master it only if we face it together. And that, my friends, is why we have the United Nations." Kofi Annan

The previous chapter, dealing with foreign policy, outlined the way in which state actors interact with the international environment. Since the Treaty of Westphalia in 1648, states have been, until relatively recently, the main actors in international relations. For much of the time between 1648 and the present day, the primary interaction between different parts of the world was done by states. However, through the 19th and 20th centuries the dominance of states in international relations has steadily declined. This resulted especially from the increase in international trade that accompanied industrialization.

According to the Union of International Associations, in the 18th century, 52 new NGOs and 4 new IGOs were founded. In the 19th century, 946 new NGOs and 94 new IGOs were begun. In the 20th century, 33,315 new NGOs, and 5725 new IGOs were established. So far, in the 21st century, 4888 new NGOs and 597 new IGOs have been created. We can therefore see a dramatic increase in the number of non-state actors, and this trend will undoubtedly continue.

In the previous chapter, we discussed polarity and polarization. One type of polarity, nonpolarity is used to describe a situation in which there are no major centers of power (i.e., states), and instead power is dispersed and diffused among many actors in the international environment. Importantly, these actors include both state actors and non-state actors. So, it is to non-state actors in international relations that we now turn.

There are two types of non-state actors: intergovernmental organizations (IGOs), and non-governmental organizations (NGOs). IGOs, such as the United Nations and the World Bank are made by states to deal with transnational issues. NGOs are private organizations made by citizens or groups of citizens, and are thus, in principle,

Chapter 10 Non-state actors in world politics

independent of the state.

IGOs vary in size and scope, according to their membership and purpose. The UN, for example, is a global IGO with 193 member states. Its purpose is extremely broad, covering global peace and security, international development and peaceful relations between member states.

The North Atlantic Treaty Organization (NATO) on the other hand, has just 28 member states in Europe and North America. Its purpose is the collective defense of its members.

The Association of South-East Asian Nations (ASEAN) comprises all of the ten states of South-east Asia. It is a regional IGO, and its purposes are to promote development, cooperation and peace in the South-East Asian region. Most IGOs focus on a limited number of cross-border issues or problems.

NGOs, like IGOs, vary greatly in size and scope. They work in every area of human activity. Advocacy NGOs such as Amnesty International work in the political arena on issues such as human rights. Businesses such as Toyota and Apple are economic entities aimed at generating profit through the provision of goods and services. Development NGOs such as Save the Children work on social issues, for example, health and education for children. Many NGOs, though not all, are part of what we call civil society, which is that part of human activity that is not controlled by the state, and that does not aim at the pursuit of economic gain or profit.

Importantly for us studying international relations, these examples of NGOs all work across national borders. They work in different locations in different countries around the world, and establish international networks to facilitate their work. Also of significance is the point that NGOs and IGOs often cooperate together. The UN, for example, maintains a huge network of thousands of NGOs, some of whom have consultative status in UN agencies.

This chapter will begin by looking at global IGOs, before moving on to smaller, regional IGOs. Then, we will look at a variety of NGOs from private business, such as multinational corporations to civil society organizations such as ethnopolitical and religious groups, and issue-advocacy and development-oriented NGOs. Finally and most importantly perhaps, we will discuss the impact of such non-state actors

131

on the traditional dominance of state actors in international relations.

10-1 Global IGOs
The United Nations

The UN is perhaps the best-known global IGO. While it was formally created in the immediate post-World War Two period (the UN Charter came into effect on the 24th of October in 1945), the name "United Nations" was first used in the 1942 "Declaration of the United Nations". This declaration was intended to unite all the Allies against the Axis Powers of Germany, Italy and Japan. According to this declaration, no member of the Allies was to attempt to make a separate peace with any of the enemy states. After this time, "United Nations" became the official name for the Allies.

Considering this background, it is understandable that the main victors of World War Two, and the United States in particular, were the primary architects of the United Nations organization. As the makers of the new organization and as the main victors of World War Two, the five states of the USA, the UK, the USSR, France and the Republic of China, gave themselves special status (to be discussed later). In 1945, 51 states joined the new United Nations organization.

Purposes and Principles

The United Nations Charter outlines its purposes and principles. Article One gives four purposes of the UN:

1. international peace and security,
2. developing and maintaining friendly relations between states based on the principles of equal rights and self-determination for all peoples,
3. to achieve international cooperation in solving international problems, and promote human rights and freedoms,
4. to be a center for encouraging harmonization between states' actions.

Article Two of the UN Charter outlines a number of key principles: equality between states, peaceful resolution of disputes, and non-interference in the domestic affairs of a state. The final one, non-interference in domestic affairs, is a core component of the principle of sovereignty, and so the UN Charter was upholding the sovereign rights of its member states.

It is entirely understandable that maintaining international peace and security was a primary aim of an institution that was made following the most destructive war in human history. However, achieving this purpose soon became complicated by the Cold War between the USA and the USSR.

Despite this, the UN became involved in developments in every corner of the globe. Indeed, the UN has attempted to deal with the dramatic increase in transnational problems in the years since the end of World War Two. These problems include development in developing countries, the spread of weapons of mass destruction, climate change and other environmental problems, dealing with health crises such as HIV/AIDS, bird flu and Ebola, and human rights abuses by member states. To deal with such a wide variety of issues, the UN has a large number of offices around the world and a complex organizational structure.

Organizational Structure

The UN Charter created six principal organs;

1. The General Assembly is the place where all member states of the UN are represented equally. This means that all member states, regardless of size, population or economic power, have one vote each. The General Assembly is the main deliberative body of the UN, meaning that issues are discussed here. The General Assembly can also vote on resolutions, but these are only recommendations.

2. The Security Council is the organ that deals with peace and security. Unlike the General Assembly, the Security Council does have the power to use force in international relations. This force usually consists of economic and other sanctions, but can include the use of military force. The Security Council has five permanent members (the USA, Russia, China, the UK and France), all of which have veto power. The veto power means that any one of these five permanent members can, by themselves, block any Security Council action. The Security Council has ten nonpermanent members who are elected by the General Assembly and who serve a two-year term.

3. The Economic and Social Council (ECOSOC) is responsible for coordinating UN development activities. Its 54 members are elected by the General Assembly for a two-year period. ECOSOC has evolved

into a forum to discuss and debate development issues. It has established a network of over 3000 NGOs who participate in a lot of the UN's development work.

4. The Trusteeship Council was set up to administer territories that had yet to achieve independence. It was thus designed to assist in the process of decolonization in the postwar era. The Trusteeship Council was disbanded in 1994, following the independence of Palau, the last of its trustee territories.

5. The International Court of Justice is the legal court of the UN. It terms of jurisdiction, it is restricted to settling disputes between states and needs the consent of states involved in the dispute before it can hear cases. It has 15 judges elected by the General Assembly and Security Council.

6. The Secretariat is the bureaucracy of the UN. It is headed by the Secretary-General, who is currently Ban Ki-moon of South Korea. Most of the UN secretariat is based in the New York headquarters of the UN.

The United Nations also has a vast array of other organizations, some under its direct control, and others that are autonomous. It may be most appropriate to think of the United Nations as similar to a family of organizations, some closely related, whilst others are more distant relations. Programs and Funds such as the United National Environmental Program (UNEP), the United Nations Development Program (UNDP), the United Nations Population Fund (UNFPA) and the World Food Program (WFP) come under the authority of the General Assembly. Other organizations such as the International Labor Organization (ILO), the World Bank Group, the International Monetary Fund (IMF) and the World Health Organization are independent organizations that have their own budgets, staff, and so on.

UN Finance and Budget

Article 17 of Chapter Four of the UN Charter states that, "The expenses of the Organization shall be borne by the Members as apportioned by the General Assembly." This means that the overall UN budget and the levels of payment for each member are to be decided by the General Assembly. In principle, each member state is to pay according to the size of that state's economy, which means of course that the richer states pay more than the poorer states.

The UN budget can be divided into three parts. The core budget covers the regular expenses of the UN Secretariat, while there is a separate peacekeeping budget and budget for voluntary programs.

The main contributors to the UN core budget of US$5.5 billion (2012-3) were the US (22%), Japan (10.8%), Germany (7%), France (5.6%), UK (5.2%), China (5.1%) and Italy (4.4%). Another ten states pay a further 21% combined, meaning that the remaining 177 relatively less wealthy states pay 18.3% of the total.

The main contributors to the UN peacekeeping budget of $7.54 billion (2013–14) were the US (28.4%), Japan (10.8%), France (7.2%), Germany (7.1%), the UK (6.7%), China (6.6%), Italy (4.4%), and Russia (3.1%). As you will see, the permanent members of the Security Council pay comparatively more for peacekeeping than for the regular budget. This is connected to the fact that they must approve all peacekeeping missions.

Budgets for other UN programs and funds are voluntary. In 2011, for example, the top five contributors to UNICEF were the US (16.9%), the UK (14.2%), Norway (11%), Japan (9.4%) and Sweden (8.6%).

The vastly unequal contributions that countries pay to the UN does, of course, reflect the reality of income inequality in the modern world. However, it has been a cause of considerable disagreement and discontent. The US for example, for years refused to pay much of its contributions to the UN. Also, Japan and Germany have long complained that their power and representation at the UN do not match their financial contributions. Other states, such as India and Brazil also say they should have a permanent seat on the Security Council. All these states argue that the current distribution of power is a relic of the end of World War Two, and is not an accurate representation of the current international environment.

It should be said that considering what is expected of it, the budget of the UN is tiny. In 2011, for example, US total public spending (federal and state) was about US$6 trillion. Japan's government spending is about US$2 trillion.

The World Trade Organization

After World War Two, with the memory of the Great Depression still fresh, the US took the lead in creating an international framework that would facilitate an expansion of global trade. The US planned to create an international trade organization within the UN, but this became too difficult. As a replacement, a number of bilateral trade agreements were incorporated into the General Agreement on Tariffs and Trade (GATT), which was supposed to be temporary.

GATT continued to promote the liberalization of global trade, until the World Trade Organization (WTO) came into existence in 1995. The WTO has the power to enforce trade rules and resolve trade disputes. In the 21st century about 30 trade disputes are brought to the WTO every year.

The primary goal of the WTO is to make a world of liberal or free trade, a world in which all states can trade freely in whatever goods or services they can provide. Of course, this is the ideal of free trade. The system of world trade we now have is far from this ideal. One of the main criticisms of the WTO is that it is undemocratic. Many major policy decisions are made by the few most powerful states in a condition of secrecy.

The World Bank

At Bretton Woods in July 1944, the World Bank (then called the International Bank for Reconstruction and Development, known as the IBRD) was established to finance the reconstruction of Europe after World War Two. In the years since then, the World Bank has evolved into the primary financier of international development. The World Bank is able to offer loans with favorable conditions to developing countries, which cannot get credit at low interest from international financial markets. Concessional loans are loans that have interest rates below that of the market, meaning that they are cheaper and easier to repay.

The World Bank has a Board of Governors, which meets annually to decide overall policy. However, the day-to-day operations of the World Bank are managed by a Board of Directors, which has 24 members. The largest contributors to the capital stock of the World Bank have their own director. They are currently the USA, UK, France, Japan, Germany, Saudi Arabia, Russia, China and Switzerland.

All other directors are chosen by groups of countries. Voting is done according to a 'weighted voting system', whereby states have voting power equal to their financial contribution. Needless to say, this

Chapter 10 Non-state actors in world politics

means that the World Bank is controlled by the rich states, and this is shown by the fact that the President of the World Bank is always an American.

Even though the World Bank began as a financial institution providing loans, it has grown into a hub of development expertise, which is at the very center of the international foreign aid system. However, it has also been heavily criticized for focusing on middle-income countries rather than the poorest countries. It has also been criticized for attaching certain conditions to its loans. Some conditions, such as those relating to corruption, seem to be rational attempts at reducing waste. Others, such as the structural adjustment conditions, seem to be following a strong political agenda. This political agenda was termed the Washington Consensus, and involved the World Bank using its financial power to force developing countries to open their markets, privatize many of their industries, and reduce their government spending. It seemed to many that the World Bank was not operating in the best interests of developing countries.

10-2 Regional IGOs

As we have seen from the cases of the IGOs mentioned in the previous section, it often seems that these organizations are working for the strongest states. Indeed, realists would argue that such strong states would always either use the IGO for their own best interests or simply ignore it. However, liberals would say that we do have one very good example where strong states have cooperated in an IGO.

The European Union

After World War Two, Europe was in ruins. Millions of Europeans had been killed in the conflict, and cities and industries had been destroyed. All of this had happened within a generation of World War One, the Great War, which had been called 'the war to end all wars'. Many Europeans felt that the best way to preserve peace in Europe was to integrate their societies and economies.

The formal process of European unification began in 1951 with the establishment of the European Coal and Steel Community (ECSC). This had been proposed by French Foreign Minister Robert Schuman, who saw it as a way to allow Germany to rebuild its heavy industry without alarming its neighbors. The coal and steel resources of France and Germany (and later Luxembourg, Belgium, the Netherlands and Italy) would be jointly managed by the ECSC. The integration of Europe continued with the formation of the European Economic Community and the European Union. The European Union has a common foreign policy and common justice policy. And with the single market, the EU also has the biggest economy in the world.

It is possible that in the future the EU will expand further, beyond its current 28 member states. One state that has been trying to join for some time is Turkey, and this has been controversial because of Turkey's position as a Muslim nation. Whilst much of Europe is now multi-cultural, it is argued that the admission of a Muslim state would fundamentally change the identity of the EU.

The dramatic expansion of the EU eastwards has caused major changes to the organization. The inflow of immigrants into the richer western economies from the poorer eastern economies has placed stress on public services, especially welfare payments. This has caused serious public debate in a number of member states, which could potentially threaten EU unity.

The EU has developed an array of institutions to manage the affairs of Europe. The Council of Europe is the key policy making institution. Cabinet Ministers from all EU member states meet here to discuss and make policy. For example, when an issue related to European farming is to be discussed, agriculture ministers from member states will meet. When military affairs need to be discussed, ministers of defense from member states will gather. Most decisions are made by a system called "qualified majority voting", which gives larger countries more votes, but not enough to allow them to dominate.

The European Commission (EC), based in Brussels, consists of twenty-eight commissioners chosen by member governments and approved by the European Parliament. Each of these commissioners (except the President), heads a department, which is like a government ministry. The EC is the executive branch of the EU. Like any executive it manages the day-to-day operations of the EU, such as proposing new laws, ensuring the implementation of EU treaties, etc. The European Civil Service is the bureaucracy for the EC, and in 2012, there were nearly 24,000 officials and other staff working in this EC.

The European Parliament is now like any other parliament in a democracy. The citizens of Europe vote directly for their

Chapter 10 Non-state actors in world politics

representatives, just as they do for their state's parliamentarians. The power of the European Parliament has increased over time, and it passes laws, approves the EU's budget and oversees the EC. However, the European Parliament is not a legislature like parliaments in most EU member states. It shares its legislative power with both the EC and the Council of the European Union.

The European Court of Justice in Luxemburg is the highest judicial power of the EU. As with most other EU institutions, it has grown in power as integration has progressed. At its beginnings, the Court dealt with disputes between member governments, and between member governments and EU institutions. However, now the Court is also involved in cases concerning individual citizens. The finding of the European Court of Justice are binding, meaning that all lower courts, including member states' supreme courts, must follow them.

The European Central Bank manages the common monetary policy of the EU. Like a national central bank, the European Central Bank sets interest rates and manages the money supply of the Euro, which is the single currency shared by a majority of the European states. Of course, the aim of having one currency throughout the EU is to make trade within the EU easier and cheaper. Each time money is converted from one currency into another, there is a transaction cost, just as when you convert your yen into dollars, or your dollars into pounds.

The elimination of national currencies may have been difficult for many citizens. It may well be that citizens have an emotional attachment to their nation's currency. However, this was just one more step in Europe's continuing integration, which can be described as the pooling of sovereignty.

In the process of pooling sovereignty, member states give up or transfer some of their power (sovereignty) to the EU. The EU pools this sovereignty together in governing the EU as a whole. The EU has taken this concept of pooled sovereignty further than any other IGO. This has required considerable political will, and the continuing Euro Crisis is a major challenge to the prospects of further integration. However, regardless of this, the EU is still regarded as a model to aspire to by other regional IGOs.

ASEAN

The Association of South-east Asian Nations was established in 1967 in Bangkok by Thailand, Indonesia, Malaysia, the Philippines and Singapore. In 1967, the US military was heavily involved in the conflict in Vietnam, which would soon spread to Laos and Cambodia. The Cultural Revolution had erupted in China, which continued to support communist insurgencies in South-east Asia. It was in this regional environment that ASEAN was created.

These founding states wanted to be able to focus on state-building and economic development, while also preventing both a communist takeover of their own state and being dragged into the expanding conflict in Vietnam. The 1967 Bangkok Declaration therefore focused on development, peace and security, and regional cooperation. It also established the system whereby the hosting of the ASEAN Summit is done on a rotation basis, whereby each member state takes turns.

Straight after gaining independence, Brunei Darussalam became the sixth member in 1984. In 1995, Vietnam became the seventh member. Laos and Myanmar joined two years later in 1997, and finally Cambodia made the organization complete by joining in 1999. East Timor submitted a letter of application in 2011, and is likely to meet the development conditions for membership in the near future.

In 1992, ASEAN established the ASEAN Free Trade Area (AFTA), the main component of which is the Common Effective Preferential Tariff (CEPT) scheme. The CEPT scheme does not apply to imports coming in to ASEAN from outside the region. According to this scheme, ASEAN member states must apply preferential tariff rates (0-5%) to imports from other member states. The purpose of this is obviously to encourage trade between ASEAN members.

The administrative structure of ASEAN is totally different to that of the EU. There is no permanent ASEAN bureaucracy, no legislature, judiciary or executive. The ASEAN Summit is attended by heads of state and is held twice a year. In 2014, the Summits were held in Nay Pyi Taw, the capital of Myanmar. At the same time as the ASEAN Summit, a number of other summits are also held with ASEAN partners, such as China, Japan and the Republic of Korea.

There are three ASEAN Community Councils, the ASEAN

Political-Security Community Council, the ASEAN Economic Community Council and the ASEAN Socio-Cultural Community Council. The relevant government minister for each member state sits on these councils.

Each member state appoints a Permanent Representative to ASEAN with the rank of Ambassador. These Representatives form the Committee of Permanent Representatives (CPR), which is based in Jakarta, Indonesia.

It seems that ASEAN is looking to the EU as a model for its own development. However, ASEAN has a long way to go. A key principle of ASEAN is non-interference in the domestic affairs of other members. In this way sovereignty is strongly protected. However, this principle is coming under pressure, and member states do sometimes comment on, or even criticize, the domestic policies of other member states. A good example of this is Myanmar, which has often caused problems for ASEAN.

Other regional IGOs

There are a number of other regional IGOs, most of which were established like the EU and ASEAN to promote trade between member states. NATO, however, is a military alliance that was created to fight the Cold War. However, with the collapse of the Soviet Union it has increased its membership and has become involved in missions outside of Europe, such as in Afghanistan.

Regional IGOs that were established to promote trade and economic integration include the Council of Arab Economic Unity (CAEU), the Caribbean Community (CARICOM), the Economic Community of West African States (ECOWAS), the Latin American Integration Association (LAIA), the South Asian Association for Regional Cooperation (SAARC), the Asia Pacific Economic Cooperation (APEC) forum, and the Southern African Development Community (SADC). As we can see, virtually every region of the world is attempting to promote trade through economic integration.

So, as we have seen, there are a large number of Intergovernmental Organizations, which can be divided into global and regional ones. The EU has achieved a level of integration that is not matched by any other IGO. There are many reasons for this, historical, political, cultural, social and economic, but it is likely that many leaders outside of Europe are unwilling to pool sovereignty to the level of that in Europe. It may be that such leaders are unwilling to give up their power, or it may be that they think their people are not yet ready for such a thing.

We have looked at just some of the major IGOs. Let us now turn to Non-governmental Organizations.

10-3 NGOs

As previously outlined, NGOs can be broadly separated into the following three groups: private businesses, civil society organizations such as ethnopolitical and religious groups, and issue-advocacy and development-oriented NGOs. However before we look at these different NGOs, it is perhaps useful to investigate why citizens form groups.

The key reason is very simple. People make groups to do something that they cannot do by themselves. A sports club is a good example. Most sports involve competition, and this requires a group of people. In private business, groups are made so as to benefit from specialization and economies of scale. Simply put, economies of scale mean that the more of a product a company produces, the cheaper the cost of each unit will be. Achieving economies of scale should allow companies to make more goods, and to sell those goods at lower prices in higher volumes, and to achieve overall increases in profit.

People make civil society organizations for the same basic reason. Whilst civil society organizations are not-for-profit, citizens make and join such groups in order to do something that they cannot do alone. This is called collective action. Citizens recognize that the power of the group is greater than the power of the individual, and so form groups. Issue-advocacy NGOs are a good example of this. Any government is highly unlikely to change its policy just because one citizen asks it to. But, if a large NGO has thousands of members, the government will listen to it and consider its opinion.

However, why are NGOs important for international relations? As previously outlined, one reason is that a large number of NGOs are international, meaning that they work across national borders in a number of different countries. Another reason is that large NGOs, such as advocacy-issue NGOs are significant actors in international regimes.

Chapter 10 Non-state actors in world politics

An international regime is a set of principles and norms, rules and procedures that guide the actions of states in relation to a particular issue area. For example, there is a human rights international regime that includes IGOs, such as the UN, international human rights law, states, and NGOs, such as Amnesty International and the International Committee of the Red Cross. The NGOs are key actors in these international regimes because they have large memberships and because they are highly professional.

From a constructivist perspective, NGOs are influential because of the power of ideas. Being highly specialized organizations, NGOs are able to generate ideas and participate in the decision making process.

Private Businesses

Often the acronym NGO is used only to refer to non-profit organizations, but here we will include private businesses in this category. It need not be said that with the growth of capitalism, and its triumph over communism, private businesses are key players in our global political economy. Multinational Corporations (MNCs) are especially important.

MNCs are companies that operate in a number of different countries. According to the United Nations Conference on Trade and Development (UNCTAD), there are 889,416 MNCs around the world (82,053 parent corporations and 807,363 affiliates). In 2008, the total sales of the top 100 MNCs was nearly $8.5 trillion, which is almost twice the size of the Japanese economy. The top 500 MNCs account for 70% of world trade, and employ millions of people around the world.

MNCs may have their headquarters in one country, research and development organizations in two or more countries, production facilities in a number of countries, and sell their products in very many different countries.

Toyota, for example, has its headquarters in Japan. However, it has research and development facilities in Europe, China, Thailand, Australia, as well as in Japan. The production of Toyota vehicles is done in 27 countries and its vehicles are sold in more than 160 countries.

Nike is another good example. It has a vast global network of manufacturing facilities: 54 in North America, 68 in Latin America, 14 in Africa, 28 in Europe, 468 in Asia and 4 in Australia.

In this way, MNCs use global commodity chains. They get their resources from a number of different countries, and before assembly of the final product, different parts are produced in different countries. Once assembled into a finished form, the product is then sold in different countries.

A good example of a global commodity chain is the production of jeans. The raw material comes from Kazakhstan, and it is manufactured in Turkey into yarn. It is colored in Taiwan, and then woven in Poland. France supplies buttons and rivets. It is then sewn together in the Philippines, before final processing is done in Greece. Lastly, it is sold in, for example, a shop in Osaka, Japan.

It used to be that all MNCs were American, European or Japanese. However, recently, the number of MNCs from the Global South, or developing countries, has increased. A notable example from South Korea is Samsung, which is now arguably producing more superior products than Japanese electronics makers. Hisense is a Chinese electronics company that makes home appliances, which had revenue of US$15.04 billion in 2013. Even though Hisense is a state-owned enterprise (SOE), it is an MNC because it has operations around the world. The Indian MNC Tata Group had revenue of US$103 billion in 2014 (58% of which came from outside India). Tata are involved in a number of industries. In 2008 Tata Motors bought Jaguar Land Rover, the British maker of luxury cars.

It also used to be the case that MNCs identified strongly with their home country. While some still do that, a large number of MNCs have now become Transnational Corporations (TNCs), which are truly global corporations. Their headquarters may even have moved from their home country. Nestle, the world's largest food maker, is a good example of a TNC, as is the oil company Royal Dutch Shell.

MNCs are often criticized for operating factories in countries that have no labor standards or environmental laws. It is also often argued that they exploit the resources of Global South countries, while exporting profits to the stockholders in the rich world. Regardless of these criticisms, MNCs and TNCs are essential to the global economy, and are therefore also important for the study of international relations.

The growth of MNCs has been greatly assisted by the growth in Transnational Banks (TNBs). TNBs are the main financial institutions in the globalized world economy. In 2006 the world's ten largest banks

Chapter 10 Non-state actors in world politics

had $12.8 trillion in assets. TNBs carry out financial transactions across national borders, and so they finance much of the world's foreign direct investment (FDI).

FDI is when a company or individual from one country invests directly in another country. China has benefited considerably from FDI, which brings in foreign technology and expertise, as well as foreign capital. In 2012, China received US$ 253 billion (18% of the world total) in FDI. In that year it received more FDI than any other country. However, nearly half of FDI went to just five countries, the other four being the US ($ 175 billion), Brazil ($ 65 billion), the United Kingdom ($ 63 billion) and France ($ 62 billion).

If we compare the revenue of corporations and the Gross National Income (GNI) of countries, then many MNCs and TNCs are, in fact, bigger than many countries. For example, in 2007, the private corporations of WalMart, Exxon Mobil, and Royal Dutch Shell had larger revenue than the GNI of Austria, Saudi Arabia, Indonesia and Norway. However, this does not mean that these corporations are more powerful than these states. States still control the power to make laws and regulations within their national borders, and have legitimate military forces.

Ethnopolitical and Religious Groups

While states are still the main actors in international relations, many people around the world identify first with a ethnopolitical or religious group. Of course, all people have multiple layers of identity, but with the rise of nationalism, many citizens began to strongly identify with their nation-state. However, in much of the world, this is not the case. The Kurds in Iraq, Turkey and Iran, for example, identify first with their ethnic group.

Importantly for the Kurds, they do not have their own state, and are spread across three states. In Myanmar, most of the ethnic groups of the mountainous border regions, such as the Shan, the Karen and the Kachin identify first with their ethnic group. Indeed, after many years of conflict, members of these groups are more likely to view the state as the enemy, rather than as "their own" state. The existence of such identities and the NGOs that they make, mean that it is difficult to view the state as a unitary actor, as realism does.

It has been estimated that there are 6,800 indigenous groups in

145

the world. Each of these groups has its own language and culture. However, the process of state building has led to the creation of fewer than 200 states. Thus it is unsurprising that many people feel that the state they live in is not really "theirs".

However, as well as ethnic identities, many people around the world also have a religious identity, and in some cases, this may be someone's first or most important identity. While it might seem that religion should cause harmony, this has not been the case.

In the Thirty Years' War (1618–1648) between Catholics and Protestants nearly a quarter of all Europeans were killed. Even today, religion plays a major role in many conflicts. Religious movements have political purposes, even though their principles and norms are based on religion. Obviously, different religions are very different in their beliefs and outlooks, and it is therefore very difficult to generalize. However, it seems that people who have strong religious beliefs often think that their beliefs are superior to others, and this causes conflict.

Islamic Fundamentalism is often cited as a example of the potential dangers of religious movements. While it is again difficult to generalize, Islamic Fundamentalist groups use certain aspects of Islam to justify their violent actions. Al Qaeda and Islamic State are two examples that vividly show the importance of such religious movements to international relations. Although we would usually include such NGOs within civil society, it is often said that groups that carry out such violent action cannot be included within a civil society. Issue-advocacy and development-oriented NGOs, in contrast, are usually part of civil society.

Issue-advocacy and development-oriented NGOs

Issue-advocacy NGOs are organizations that focus on specific issue areas. They campaign for particular action connected to that issue area, and can develop into highly professional organizations. Needless to say, such NGOs need political space to operate in. Political space means the freedom to take collective action that is political, such as publishing reports or organizing peaceful demonstrations. Liberal democracies provide the best environment for such action. In fact, it is probable that such NGOs are an essential part of the democratic process because they empower ordinary citizens, allowing them to participate in politics.

Chapter 10 Non-state actors in world politics

Greenpeace has been a prominent NGO since the 1960s. It has campaigned on issues ranging from nuclear testing, whaling and pollution. In 2011, it had a budget of €236.9 million, and a staff of 2,400. Its head office is in Amsterdam, but it has offices around the world. Greenpeace has nearly 3 million members. Greenpeace is famous for its direct action, examples of which are the attempts by Greenpeace boats to save individual whales by moving between the whaling boat and the whale. Actions such as this mean that Greenpeace is often in the news, and this helps it to gain supporters, and to mobilize public opinion for particular causes.

Some NGOs have become increasingly prominent in international development, including humanitarian assistance. These NGOs, such as the Red Cross, Médecins Sans Frontières / Doctors Without Borders (MSF), and Save the Children operate and raise funds in many countries.

Importantly, state development agencies, such as the British Department for International Development (DfID), the Japan International Cooperation Agency (JICA), and IGOs such as UNDP and the World Bank, are all increasing their cooperation with NGOs. This means that NGOs can receive public funds from state or IGO sources. Some NGOs however, refuse to accept funding from the state, arguing that their financial independence from the state is important for them to be able to carry out their missions.

It is difficult to conclude that these NGOs are crucial actors in international relations. Certainly they have a voice, and certainly they are able to participate in the decision making process. In this way, they have some power and some influence. Track II diplomacy, carried out by non-government officials, scientist, NGOs, etc., can often be complementary to the more traditional Track I diplomacy done by government officials. This is because in Track II the people have more freedom to exchange ideas. The 1993 Oslo Accords between Israel and the Palestine Liberation Organization(PLO) are often cited as an example of successful track two diplomacy. It is likely that states will use NGOs when they can, ignore them when they can, and listen to them when they have to.

10-4 A non-polar world?

So, does the existence of all these non-state actors mean that the power of states is decreasing? Is the world entering a period of non-polarity where states are no longer able to dominate?

Realists argue that IGOs and NGOs are of little importance to international relations. In high politics issue areas such as security, states still dominate. In low politics areas such as environmental issues, states allow NGOs to participate. Liberals and Constructivists disagree with this. They argue that IGOs and NGOs are important because of the multiple connections between different societies and because of the importance of ideas. States are being challenged from above, by MNCs and TNCs, and from below, by civil society organizations such as NGOs. It is also likely that many IGOs will become more and more independent of states over time.

It is possibly best to think of states as being one prominent member of a web of relationships that include IGOs and NGOs. In this way, states are still a dominant force, but they are no longer alone in having power in international relations.

P.S.

Questions

1. *Intergovernmental organizations are neutral actors, independent of the states that created them. Discuss.*

2. *The United Nations is a mirror of world politics, not an alternative to it. Discuss.*

3. *The United Nations needs to be dramatically reformed to be effective.*

4. *Are religious movements a source of conflict or harmony in international relations?*

5. *In order to understand all transnational problems, it is necessary to study non-state actors. Discuss.*

Afterword: Looking back, and looking forward

"Tomorrow belongs to those who prepare for it today." Malcolm X.

In our first chapter, we considered how the world has changed and how the world has remained the same. Despite the quite amazing technological progress of recent history, many things remain the same. Even though many areas of the world enjoy a prosperous and peaceful life, other areas endure poverty and conflict. Many of these areas of poverty have changed little. However, many areas that were once poor are now relatively rich.

When we study an event in international relations, it is necessary for us to use theoretical frameworks and models. These help us to understand the complex world by simplifying it so that we can focus on particular aspects.

The three levels of analysis are a very useful tool for studying international relations. Using it, we can look at an international event from the system level, from the state level, and from the individual level. Each of these levels can give us access to a different perspective, a different lens through which to view the event. If we use the three levels of analysis, we can get a more complete understanding. We are less likely to miss some important information.

We also looked at proximate and remote causes. This is a useful way to differentiate causes of events in international relations. Proximate causes are those causes that are recent, while remote causes are those that happened some time ago. We must be careful not to miss these causes. If we miss, then we could misunderstand the causes of an event in international relations. History is an important part of international relations!

While the three levels of analysis provides a kind of model or framework we can use to help us understand events and issues in international relations, we must be careful when using such models. These models are useful, even essential, but they have their limitations. Because they simplify the world, they pass over some information. Maps are two-dimensional models of the world that we can use to

Afterword: Looking back, and looking forward

illustrate this idea. Some maps show countries, some maps show geographical features (mountains, rivers, etc.), and some maps show ethnic groups. All of these maps focus on something. But all of them also ignore many features of the world. Models contain the same risk-- in simplifying the world so that we can understand it, we may inadvertently erase or ignore points that are actually vital.

There are also another set of dangers for us to be aware of, and these dangers are within our own mind. They concern the way that we humans think, and so are psychological characteristics. Basically, we humans often have biased perception. Of course, all humans have roughly the same senses of perception, and so perceive the same things. However, our perception is not objective and neutral, but comes with built-in default settings.

In our brain these default settings are decided by our socialization and our experience. When our eyes see something new, our brain uses its default settings to try to understand this new thing. This can lead to mistakes. It is very important for us to understand these perception biases so that we can overcome them. if we want to truly understand, we must overcome these biases. In chapter one, we looked at confirmation bias, cognitive dissonance, attribution bias and schematic reasoning. These are connected to prejudices and stereotypes that become part of our brain's default setting.

In chapter two, we looked at the idea of sovereignty. This is a key concept in international relations. Indeed, it is one of the most important pillars of our international system. Sovereignty can be thought of as a right of states. Just as we individuals have certain rights, so too do states. In international relations, states have the right to independence and autonomy. Very simply, this means that states have the right to decide what happens within their territory. However, in human history, states are relatively new, and certainly our global system of sovereign states is very new. The 1648 Treaty of Westphalia established the system of states in Europe, although it was really the end of colonialism especially after the second world war that saw this system become a global system.

Nationalism was a phenomenon that arose with the rise of the state system. In our 21st century globalized world, nationalism is now viewed negatively, but it was necessary for building these new states. Citizens within these states needed a new identity that would connect

151

them to the state.

Alongside this new international political system arose an international economic system. This economic system is capitalism, which is based on the free exchange of goods and services in the market. Free does not mean things have no price. Rather, it means things are freely exchanged at a price set by the market, and not (generally) by the state. In capitalist systems, citizens have private property rights, and this means they can become wealthy. It also means that the law will protect the property of citizens. With imperialism, capitalism spread around the world to become the international capitalist economy that we now call the global economy.

In chapter three, we discussed the 20th century history of international relations, beginning with the rise of liberalism after World War One. The first 'industrial war' was so terrible that people called it, "the war to end all wars". After the war, leaders tried to create an international order based on law and justice, and not on power. But, the new League of Nations was powerless to stop aggression, and the Great Depression caused states to become less economically dependent on each other. Realists criticized the utopian idea of liberals as dangerously unrealistic. World War Two seemed to support the view of realists. In the post-World War two world, the Cold War caused the rise of Neo-realism, while the increase in economic interdependence and international cooperation caused the rise of neo-liberalism. In many ways, the 20th century was a continuous struggle between realism and liberalism. However, there were also other theories of international relations. Among these were international society, constructivism, Marxism and feminism. All play an important role in the study of international relations.

In chapter four, we discussed classical realism, with its focus on human nature. Even though neo-realism kept most of the assumptions of realism, the focus shifted slightly to the anarchy of the world system. we then discussed the policies that realists tend to support. The key point is the primary importance given to national security, and the need for a strong military. While international cooperation is limited in realism, this is not just because of the self-help principle. It is also because of the realists worry about relative gains. This means that, even though international cooperation will result in mutual gains, realists worry that others gain more.

Afterword: Looking back, and looking forward

In chapter five, we looked at liberalism, which is based on the principle of individual liberty, or freedom. In international relations, liberalism assumes that humans can and do cooperate. Liberalism also believes in the importance of economic interdependence. This interdependence will make war less likely because war is bad for trade. Liberalism also believes in the ability of international institutions to support peace. This is because international institutions are places to discuss and to cooperate.

In chapter six, we looked at Marxism and Neo-Marxism. These stress the importance of economic inequality in the international capitalist system, and argue that groups exploit other groups for their own profit. Lenin argued that imperialism was a natural result of the capitalist system. Dependency theory is a more modern version of Marxism and believes that the international system is controlled by the rich countries in the center, and that poor countries cannot escape from their poverty in the periphery. World Systems analysis is similar in many ways, but does recognize that countries are able to move from the periphery to semi-periphery and the center.

In chapter seven we looked at the way in which societies are constructed. Societies are made and remade over time. In just the same way, international society, the society of international relations is also made and remade over time. For constructivism, ideas and identity are important. Ideas make societies and new ideas remake societies. We could say that ideas shape society. In the same way, identity shapes the way people act in society. People act in society according to their view of themselves, their identity. We should say, of course, that people have a number of identities. Importantly too, these identities are made in the interaction between individuals and their society. An important example we used in this textbook was of the change from a Sinocentric world to a Eurocentric world in East Asia. In a Sinocentric world, the ideas and identities of China were primary, while in the Eurocentric world, our world, the ideas and identities originating in Europe are primary.

In chapter eight we looked at feminism, and its importance to international relations. We discussed how gender roles are constructed and how these affect behavior. From a feminist perspective, the dominance of men in positions of power has an important impact on international relations. For example, feminists argue that anarchy and self-help (two key concepts in realism) are concepts made by men, and that this is revealed in the dominant understandings of these concepts. Furthermore, the rational economic actor, who is so important in liberalism is not a naturally occurring human, but is in fact a capitalist invention who tends to be male more than female.

In chapter nine, we looked at how foreign policy is made by state actors. We used the three levels of analysis to discuss the different influences on foreign policy making. At the system level, polarity and polarization are used to describe the distribution of power within the international system. Also, geopolitics shows the importance of geography for foreign policy, as the geographical location of a country will influence its foreign policy choices. From the state level of analysis, the level of economic development will affect the resources and interests of a state. The amount of military power will also affect foreign policy. The type of government is important because different government systems work in different ways. Finally, there are a whole set of institutional factors that influence foreign policy making. This is because government institutions, or bureaucracies, tend to work in certain ways, and have certain weaknesses. Finally, from the individual level of analysis we can understand how the character of the leaders will affect foreign policy. While we expect our leaders to act in a rational manner, there are a number of factors which often make this impossible. Leaders often have limited time to make a decision, and they always have less than perfect information. Both of these factors result in leaders making decisions that are less than optimal.

Finally, in chapter ten, we looked at the role of non-state actors in international relations. The number of non-state actors rose dramatically in the 20th century, and this trend will surely continue. There are an increasing number of issues in international relations in which non-state actors play an important role. Firstly, we looked at the global intergovernmental organizations, the United Nations, the World Trade Organization and the World Bank. These are all key actors in certain issue areas in international relations. Secondly, we looked at the regional intergovernmental organizations, focusing on the European Union and the Association of South-east Asian Nations. Following this, we looked at the role of non-state actors which (unlike IGOs that are made by states) are made by citizens. Private business organizations and multinational corporations in particular, play a very important role in our globalized economy. Following this, we looked at ethnopolitical and religious groups that play a role in international relations. A large number of people in the world have identities connected to such groups, rather than identities connected to a state. Issue-advocacy and development-oriented NGOs have become very prominent in certain issue areas. They sometimes challenge states, and are often grassroots organizations. To conclude chapter eleven, we discussed whether the rise of such non-state actors will eventually lead to the end of the modern state system. It is unlikely that this will happen soon, but it is certainly true that non-state actors can be important for understanding international relations.

So, this textbook has given you an introduction to the field of international relations. You now have the necessary tools for analyzing events and issues in international relations. This is Part One. Part Two will deal with some specific issues in international relations, such as security, human rights, trade, and the environment.

P.S.

The authors

Patrick Strefford teaches International Development and Japanese Foreign Aid (ODA). He holds degrees in Geography (Hull), Asian Studies (Leeds), and International Politics (Kobe).

Noah McCormack teaches Comparative Culture, Sociology of Japan, and Women's Studies. He holds degrees in French (ANU), International Relations (Ritsumeikan), and modern Japanese history (ANU).

They both teach at Kyoto Sangyo University in Kyoto, Japan, and prepared this textbook for a joint International Relations course.

International Relations
A Concise Introduction

Copyright ©2015 by Noah Y. McCormack, Patrick W. Strefford
All rights reserved.
No part of this publication may be reproduced, stored in a retrieval system, or transmitted in any form or by any means, electronic, mechanical, photocopying, recording, or otherwise, without the prior permission of the publisher.

Published in Japan.   ISBN978-4-86584-014-8

For information contact : BookWay
ONO KOUSOKU INSATSU CO.,LTD.
62, HIRANO-MACHI, HIMEJI-CITY, HYOGO 670-0933 JAPAN
(Phone) 079-222-5372 (Fax) 079-244-1482